Wisdom 2

In Real Life and Management

Kochouseph Chittilappilly

Viva Books

New Delhi | Mumbai | Chennai | Kolkata | Bengaluru | Hyderabad | Kochi | Guwahati

Publisher's note

Every possible effort has been made to ensure that the information contained in this book is accurate at the time of going to press, and the publisher and author cannot accept responsibility for any errors or omissions, however caused. No responsibility for loss or damage occasioned to any person acting, or refraining from action, as a result of the material in this publication can be accepted by the editor, the publisher or the author.

Every effort has been made to trace the owners of copyright material used in this book. The author and the publisher will be grateful for any omission brought to their notice for acknowledgement in the future editions of the book.

Copyright © Viva Books Private Limited

All rights reserved. No part of this book may be reproduced, stored in a retrieval system, or transmitted in any form or by any means, electronic, mechanical, photocopying, recorded or otherwise, without the written permission of the publisher.

First Published 2012
Reprinted 2013, 2014

Viva Books Private Limited

- 4737/23, Ansari Road, Daryaganj, New Delhi 110 002
  Tel. 42242200, 23258325, 23283121, Email: vivadelhi@vivagroupindia.net

- 76, Service Industries, Shirvane, Sector 1, Nerul, Navi Mumbai 400 706
  Tel. 27721273, 27721274, Email: vivamumbai@vivagroupindia.net

- Jamals Fazal Chambers, 26 Greams Road, Chennai 600 006
  Tel. 28294241, 28290304, Email: vivachennai@vivagroupindia.net

- B-103, Jindal Towers, 21/1A/3 Darga Road, Kolkata 700 017
  Tel. 22816713, Email: vivakolkata@vivagroupindia.net

- 7, GF, Sovereign Park Aptts., 56-58, K. R. Road, Basavanagudi, Bengaluru 560 004
  Tel. 26607409, Email: vivabangalore@vivagroupindia.net

- 101-102, Moghal Marc Apartments, 3-4-637 to 641, Narayanguda, Hyderabad 500 029
  Tel. 27564481, Email: vivahyderabad@vivagroupindia.net

- First Floor, Beevi Towers, SRM Road, Kaloor, Kochi 682 018
  Tel. 0484-2403055, 2403056, Email: vivakochi@vivagroupindia.net

- 232, GNB Road, Beside UCO Bank, Silpukhuri, Guwahati 781 003
  Tel. 0361-2666386, Email: vivaguwahati@vivagroupindia.net

www.vivagroupindia.com
ISBN: 978-81-309-2119-8

Edited by:
Prof. T.P. Antony

Illustrated by
Prakash Shetty

Published by Vinod Vasishtha for Viva Books Private Limited, 4737/23 Ansari Road, Daryaganj, New Delhi 110 002.

Printed and bound by Raj Press, R-3, Inderpuri, New Delhi 110 012.

M0200/M0457/M0454/M0350

Dedication

To All First Generation Entrepreneurs.

The proceeds from the sale of this book will be utilized by me only for charitable purposes.

– *Kochouseph Chittilappilly*

Table of Contents

	Foreword	*vii*
	Preface	*ix*
1.	Complain Less, Success Will Follow	1
2.	The pitfalls of Indian democracy	4
3.	Value in practising ethical business	7
4.	The Right Attitude Propels Growth Part I	9
5.	The Right Attitude Propels Growth Part II	12
6.	Entrepreneur's role in Advertising	15
7.	Dishonesty never pays	17
8.	Give and Take	19
9.	Positive Attitude Matters	21
10.	As our thoughts change, our lives change	23
11.	A Rigid Mind Helps None	25
12.	Strength in Unity	27
13.	The Power of Motivation	29
14.	Don't underestimate anyone	31
15.	Self-Transformation furthers Development	33
16.	The 4 C's of Effective Communication	35
17.	People Management	37
18.	Strong values build strong Teams	39
19.	Leadership Success	41
20.	Keep an Open Mind	43
21.	Hard Work Pays	45
22.	Flexibility in decision making	47
23.	Learn to Lead	49
24.	Commonsense is quite uncommon	51
25.	Delegation paves the way to success	53
26.	Introspection Leads to Success	55
27.	Empowerment	57

28.	Think before you leap	59
29.	Everything is not what it appears	61
30.	Seize every opportunity	63
31.	One's Fate lies in One's own Hands	65
32.	The IPO Challenge	67
33.	Worrying breeds ill-health	69
34.	Persevere and Win	71
35.	Curiosity helps Innovate	73
36.	Effective Communication	75
37.	Presence of Mind	77
38.	Calm in a Storm	79
39.	Knock at all doors, armed with a warm heart	81
40.	Professional Commitment	84
41.	The Conquest of Fear	87
42.	Lessons from the recession	89
43.	Synergy I	91
44.	Synergy II	93
45.	Effective Delegation	95
46.	Coping with grief	98
47.	A need for Civic Sense	100
48.	Declining Spiritual Values	102
49.	Faith & Hope Part I	105
50.	Faith & Hope Part II	108
51.	Faith & Hope Part III	110
52.	Little drops of water create an ocean	113
53.	Freedom with Responsibility	115
54.	The Secret of Good Health	117
55.	My Role Models I	119
56.	My Role Models II	121
57.	The Whole Picture	123
58.	Happiness Lies Within I	125
59.	Happiness Lies Within II	127
60.	Honesty Pays	129
	About the Author	131

Foreword

Simple yet worthy in content. This book 'Practical Wisdom' by Kochouseph Chittilappilly transcends several traps to which business and management practitioners often fall prey in the milieu of Kerala's unique socio-economic, cultural and political fabric.

Aristotle once said, "For the things we have to learn before we can do them, we learn by doing them". This book is a fine dossier and a reckoner of such an 'experiential learning' - an account of leadership and practical management wisdom through the lenses of a successful entrepreneurs experience and perspectives. Through the conversation between the stories and illustrations, this book might well awaken several truths in the minds of the reader. Most, if not all, will gain amusing insights through what lies within; these collection of anecdotal stories. This book for a wider variety of reasons is thus, a reader's delight.

The most obvious and in many ways, the most enjoyable interaction that the author will quicken in you is the realistic and practical wisdom he gained from his personal, professional and social experiences. He dares to challenge some of the conventional thoughts, and insists the need for an innovative and creative social 'attitude' for entrepreneurship. In this book there is no dearth of ideas; which dwells around his urge and convictions for humane, ethical and moral values in life and business. The voluntary donation of one of his kidney to a needy in February 2011 also stands a testimony to this fact. The sweat and sacrifice of this gentleman would never go unrecognized, as he is a businessman who has invested flesh and blood for illuminating those enduring values of life.

In short, this is a useful read especially for all those in the business and in the management domain who believe in wealth creation through love and selfless service. Hope and wish Kochouseph will enlighten us with more such thoughts and creations in the years to come.

Debashis Chatterjee
Director, IIM Kozhikode

Preface

It should be noted with genuine gratitude that my earlier venture 'Practical Wisdom – 1' has received a warm welcome from the public, especially from those who have engaged in the business and management spheres. This positive response prompted me to think about the subject in greater detail so that I might cater to the need of the times as best as I can, by sharing my first hand experience and innovative experiments in this vast and dynamic field. I sincerely hope that this humble effort will help clear some misconceptions and apprehensions of many an upstart who seek to try his/her luck in the ever-enhancing horizon of business enterprises and management. I have just tried to unravel the secrets of success in this sphere, based on my own practical experiences.

Kochouseph Chittilapilly

1
Complain Less, Success Will Follow

During a training programme called 'Interacting with an Entrepreneur', held at a Management college, I was sharing my thoughts with the students, when one of them asked me, 'Can you identify the major qualities required for a leader or a successful man in any walk of life?' Although I was not quite prepared to answer this important question, I managed to put together some points and respond to it. But I was not fully satisfied with my answer. From that day, I reflected on the subject and tried to identify the qualities that would correctly define such a person.

You may have noticed that all highly intelligent people are not successful in life. At the same time, many unassuming people of average intelligence become good leaders in their own fields. So, intelligence is not the only pre-requisite for success, although it is an

> An inferiority complex suppresses one's own hidden talents.

important factor. I observed people to help me get an answer to this question. I noticed that all successful personalities had some important qualities in common.

Similarly when we look into the lives of unsuccessful people, we see that they lack certain essential qualities, which account for their failure to excel.

From my observations of people over the last several years, I am convinced that those who are successful in life, have a harmonious combination of some special qualities. Of these, I feel that developing a habit of not complaining, criticizing and condemning someone or something, is the most outstanding characteristic. I believe that this is the foundation on which we can build a successful career even if we have several setbacks. We often hear people complaining 'I was born in a poor family', 'My health is very poor'; 'The government is totally inefficient', 'Trade unions are impeding industrial growth', 'Our educational system is not purposeful' and so on. My point is that with the available facilities in our country many people have come up in their lives and are excelling in their professions. How far Is their success based on luck? Personally speaking, luck plays only a minor role in anyone's success. Good luck may prevail one day and the very next day, there could be ill-luck. So how can we rely on this evasive factor? In my view, it is foolish to do so. Everything depends on our attitude.

I watched a TV programme, which showed a handicapped musician playing the guitar with his toes as he had no hands. He is quite a celebrity in the U.S. He was born without hands; he has only a 10 cm protrusion from the shoulders. Seated on a chair, with the guitar on the floor, he played it fast with his toes, to create wonderful harmony on the guitar strings! Thousands are attracted to his musical concerts. When the TV crew interviewed him, I realized the secret of his success. He remained very cheerful and happy throughout the interview, never complaining about or cursing his handicap. Instead, he said it was a blessing in disguise for him to be without hands. He did not hesitate to say that if he had been born with both hands and had played the guitar he would have been one like any other guitarist; nobody would have noticed him as there were many guitarists even more capable and talented than him. He said that he was the happiest person in the world, with a wife and two kids.

This is a clear example of how one's attitude makes a difference in life. Many people in tough situations curse their fate and lead unproductive lives, condemning themselves and others alike. An inferiority complex suppresses one's own hidden talents. So if you want to be a successful person, never complain, criticize or condemn.

2
The pitfalls of Indian democracy

I was one of the three speakers at a seminar, where the topic of discussion was, 'Entrepreneur driven Indian Economy'. On receiving the invitation to speak at the seminar, I collected my thoughts on the subject and began to analyze why the Indian Economy has not done well, even 56 years after Independence. Everyone knows that while Indians work hard and fare extremely well outside India, they are inclined to be lazy in their own country, as a result of which, India, as a whole, remains backward. We know that small and medium scale industries are the backbone of any economy, yet Indian entrepreneurs,

> Unless we work hard and excel in our respective areas of activities, we will be side-tracked.

It was believed that a rich man could not enter heaven

with few exceptions, do not have world-class competence. I think the main reason is that the majority of our political leaders who held the reins of the government of India during the early decades of independence believed that Socialism would be a better path to progress for a poor country like India. Although we had a mixed economy, we leaned more towards the USSR than to the U.S.A. We believed that Public Sector Undertakings (PSU's) would provide the thrust needed to improve our economy. In fact, even in schools and colleges, teachers and professors would cry out that the PSU's were our national wealth and that we needed more of them.

While I was at college, when Mrs. Indira Gandhi was Prime Minister, 14 Scheduled Banks were nationalised with the intention that the government should have more control over the economy. Many multinationals were thrown out of the country, and we continued to believe that socialism was the true saviour because the USSR was then a shining example of the success of Socialism. Kerala went one step further. We introduced land reforms and we taught our youth that private wealth creation is sinful, and that 'profit' is a dirty word. For the first time in the history of the whole world, a communist ministry, elected through democratic process, came into power in Kerala in 1957. While I was a student, one of the popular political slogans was, "നമ്മൾ കൊയ്യും വയലെല്ലാം നമ്മുടേതാകും പൈങ്കിളിയേ". which means "paddy field workers dream of the day when they would own the fields in which they toiled". It was a widely held belief that the forcible and equitable distribution of wealth was necessary in order to eradicate poverty.

Even religious leaders and social reformers were all against wealth creation. I still remember that, during Sunday sermons, the priest would highlight the evils of wealth. Even the Bible says that it is more difficult for a wealthy man to enter heaven than for a camel to pass through the eye of a needle. Union leaders portrayed entrepreneurs as bloodsuckers who exploited workers. They taught our workers to disrespect the employer and to disregard work, even though according to Indian tradition, 'Work is Worship'. With an eye on the vote banks, the various governments that came into power vied with one another in enacting pro-labour laws in the name of security to the working class. The labourers were eager to assert their rights but were thoroughly indifferent to their obligations. This led to the creation of a workforce that was lethargic, less productive and less competent. Curiously enough, when the same people go abroad to work, they adapt themselves to the work culture there, which compels them to work hard and excel in their jobs. Survival of the fittest is the law of nature. It is applicable to workers, employers, organisations and the country as a whole. Unless we work hard and excel in our respective areas of activities, we will be unable to compete with the rest of the world.

3

Value in practising ethical business

Not too long ago, educated youngsters tended to prefer government jobs which were safe and secure, and were less inclined to venture to become small-scale industrialists. Once they get government jobs, they believe that their future is secure, and do not feel the need to work hard or excel. Look at the state of our government establishments. Government employees believe as a rule, that they have the freedom to inconvenience the public, and do not feel accountable to anyone. Once I met a youngster, who had secured good marks in his degree examinations. he expressed an earnest desire to get a government job. When I asked him why he wished to join the government service, he replied without hesitation that the work load would be much less, he could avail of unlimited leave, promotion would be on the basis of seniority, not efficiency and security of his tenure would be assured.

Here in India, we have countless rules and regulations, which have brought the disrepute of license Raj to the government.

> We have an increasing number of educated businessmen who are governed by values and principles in their lives.

Value in Practising Ethical Business

Excessive regulations have led to more corruption and we bear the shame of being one of the most corrupt countries in the world. Those who are straightforward and wish to retain their self-esteem, find it very difficult to do business in India. At the same time, India is a fertile land for those who are crooked, those who adopt improper methods, and for those who are ready to engage in unethical practices. For all these reasons, with very few exceptions, people with good academic credentials, ethics and self-esteem, shy away from becoming entrepreneurs. I still remember an occasion when a group of youngsters asked me "Why do you pay correct taxes to the government when the vast majority of businessmen do not? Is it because you are patriotic, or for any other reason?" I replied, "More than patriotism, I value my self-esteem, and don't wish to grovel before any official. I prefer to do business the ethical way, and I value peace of mind and happiness more than money. I want to sleep peacefully at night".

It augurs well for the future of our country that we have an increasing number of educated businessmen who are governed by values and principles in their lives. Nowadays, youngsters have real role models in Sri. Narayanamurthy and many others like him. Son of a schoolteacher from a poor family, Sri Murthy started Infosys with the meagre investment of a few thousand rupees that he managed to muster up by selling his wife Sudha Murthy's gold ornaments. Today he is one of the most respected and flourishing businessmen in India, and it should be said to his credit that he has achieved this by sticking to ethical business strategies. Our country needs more 'Narayanamurthys' to solve our chronic problem of unemployment, and to boost the economy. It is a positive sign, that as a result of the liberalization, many educated and principled youngsters are now venturing into ethical business activities. So, for all these reasons, I am extremely hopeful that India will be a developed nation by 2020 and become an economic superpower by 2040. Let us all work together and make this dream a reality.

4

The Right Attitude Propels Growth Part I

During my visit to China, I realised that the country is now far, far ahead of India in many respects. In college we were taught that China was a poor and underdeveloped country like India, with a very large population. Contrary to our expectations, what we saw in the three major cities of Shanghai, Beijing and Guangzhou (Canton) and their suburbs, were unmistakable signs of real economic growth, comparable to that of any of the developed countries. I was truly astonished to see the developments in their infrastructure. To cite but one instance, they

> In many cases the public tends to take a negative attitude, not intentionally, but out of ignorance.

now have 30,000 kms. of world class express highways connecting their major cities.

One of our vendors there, who supplies us components for some of our products, took us to his factory, situated 140 kms from Shanghai City. We travelled on the express highway, a journey which took us only one hour and twenty minutes to reach our destination. He paid a toll of 70 Yuan for using the expressway (one way), which is equivalent to approximately Rs 400/-. In view of the ongoing debate in Kerala about express highways, I was a little curious to know his impartial opinion on the matter. With a great deal of enthusiasm, he explained, "Ten years ago, my place was just like a village, before the express highway came into existence. There were not many factories, and very few buildings or good houses. In those days, it used to take us more than three hours to travel from our place to Shanghai city because of bad roads. Today, our place is virtually a part of Shanghai City."

When I enquired about his willingness to pay the relatively high sum of Rs. 400 as toll, he said, "I save a good amount on petrol and can drive non stop at a speed of 120 Km. Moreover, there are four of us in this car and I feel that 70 Yuan is negligible, considering how much of our precious time we have been able to save. In fact, I am highly obliged to the express highway because today my village has become a township and part of Shanghai City, which benefits my business greatly. After this highway came into existence, many industries were started in this area, which reduced unemployment to zero. In fact, we are dependent on other provinces to cope with our requirement of workers. Today we can't imagine life without this express highway." After hearing all these positive factors of having express highways, I felt sad thinking of the hostile attitude of the people of Kerala to the proposed express high way, totally oblivious to its benefits.

When I see the agitations and the propaganda against the proposed express highway, I am reminded of a similar situation in India, prior to Independence. When the British authorities decided to introduce railway in India, the people here opposed the move, thinking that only the British would have that facility. At that time, the local people had the notion that it would be a luxury, which would cause a lot of inconvenience to the ordinary people. But time has proved them wrong. If we analyze the matter impartially now, history appears to be repeating itself in the ongoing agitation against the proposed Express highway in Kerala. In many cases the public take a negative attitude, not intentionally, but out of ignorance. Those who have travelled abroad widely, will vouch for the fact that infrastructural facilities like express highways and bridges are the backbone of any civilized nation, and if there are private companies ready to invest in such projects, we must welcome them whole-heartedly.

5
The Right Attitude Propels Growth Part II

While we were travelling through the express highway in China, I made a few quick mental calculations of the distances involved while travelling in Kerala. Palakkad and Kollam are approximately 140 Km from Kochi. Imagine being able to reach these places in one hour and twenty minutes, effectively making them part of Kochi city! Now it takes around three hours to reach there. Furthermore, the vehicle population is growing at a fast pace. A recent study reveals that the number of vehicles on the roads in Kerala grows by roughly 13.5% per

> Infrastructure development projects will generate enormous employment opportunities in a variety of trades.

year, which means that within five years, the total number of vehicles in Kerala would double and create huge traffic jams. We now have all types of new generation cars, buses and trucks, but because of the bad, narrow and crooked roads, their usefulness and efficiency remains under-utilized. On account of traffic blocks we are compelled to drive slowly, wasting a great deal of petrol and diesel. Please remember that India spends huge amounts of foreign exchange to import crude oil, which is inevitably going to cost more in the days to come.

Those who are against a new express highway in Kerala, suggest that the existing highways can be widened to handle six line traffic, which is clearly not practical. Many shops, places of worship and other buildings along the way, will have to be demolished in this case, and the value of land to be acquired will be very high. Moreover, there are numerous small roads that directly join the existing highway at various points of entry, which again, will defeat the purpose of an expressway. According to international standards, an express highway should have only one major point of entry, located at every fifty or sixty kms. Overbridges or underpasses must be provided to cross the local roads wherever needed. And if we have a good number of them along the way, then the argument that Kerala will be divided lengthwise into two, will hold no water. I firmly believe that North Kerala will be benefited more by having an express highway. Tourism, the only one industry which is flourishing in Kerala, is now largely confined to the central and southern parts of our state. An express highway will ensure the development of tourism in north Kerala as well.

It is well that we recollect the folly that we once committed. That the Keralites objected to the introduction of tractors in our paddy fields in the 1960's and 70's, when they were being widely used in the other states of India is indeed a black chapter in Kerala history. We have only ourselves to blame for the poor state of food grain production in the State. Again, in the 80's when computers were introduced, we saw protests and agitations on a massive scale by the employees of banks, insurance companies, and civil servants, who feared that it would curtail job opportunities. I recall my father telling me that in the 50's he had witnessed agitations by bullock cart operators and their employees when goods were first transported from Trichur market to Parappur village by trucks. When I see the agitations against the express highway, I wonder whether we are repeating the same blunder!

It may be due to ignorance that many of us are now protesting against a proposal that would open the gateway to the multifarious development of our state. Moreover, I believe that we are doing injustice to the large group of unemployed youth in our state. Infrastructure development projects will generate enormous employment in a variety of trades.

6

Entrepreneur's role in Advertising

During a seminar on 'Brand Building', I had an opportunity to share some of my thoughts on this subject with others. The participants were mainly marketing managers, professionals from advertising agencies and entrepreneurs. When I addressed the audience, I had in mind the entrepreneurs, who attended the seminar. I felt that even though good advertising agencies can be useful, it is the duty of the entrepreneur or marketing manager to burn the midnight oil and chalk out new ideas in advertising and marketing schemes. In my view, the role of an advertising agency is similar to that of a gynecologist who facilitates delivery. The process of conceiving the idea itself and deciding the advertisement's intention and target audience, must come from the entrepreneur or manager. A gynecologist advises and helps the expectant mother to deliver a healthy baby. But it is the mother who has to take all the trouble to deliver and nurse the baby. A similar situation can be seen when we take a closer look at the roles played by entrepreneurs and advertising agencies.

I emphasized this aspect because I remembered a casual remark once made by someone who did not know much about business. He stated, "If you engage good advertising agencies and consultants in various fields, you need not worry about your business because the profits will flow automatically". I chose to differ from him on this

> The product's true qualities must always be correctly portrayed in its advertisements.

Entrepreneur's role in Advertising

point, and said, "Regardless of the reputation of the consultants we engage, it is our responsibility as businessmen, to do our homework very seriously, and this has been my experience". When the participants heard what I said, during the question and answer session a few of them strongly objected to my views, saying that I was underestimating the role of advertising agencies in brand building. I told them that I was not discounting the efforts and contributions of these agencies, but only emphasizing the importance of the role of the entrepreneur in that crucial process.

Recently, I noticed an advertisement of an amusement park in a South Indian city, claiming to be 'India's answer to Disneyland'. Drawn by that advertisement, and believing its substance almost blindly, I was curious to know more. I took a lot of trouble to visit that park but the visit turned out to be totally disappointing! I felt cheated when I saw that this park was nowhere near Disneyland in terms of quality, technology, size, beauty, cleanliness and service. In fact, I am sure that all those who have visited Disneyland, before visiting this park, would have left the place with the same impression that I had. As the operator of one of the largest amusement parks in India, I can honestly say that none of the amusement parks here measure up to Disneyland in many respects. I am reminded here of what John the Baptist says in the Bible about Christ, "I am not worthy to untie the straps of His sandals." I know that Veega Land and Wonder la stand in no comparison to Disneyland.

In fact, whenever our advertising agency brought me an idea for an advertisement campaign which was grossly exaggerated, I rejected it straightaway.

To sum up, customers should not feel that they have been cheated or lured into buying a product by unfounded claims. The product's true qualities must always be truthfully portrayed in its advertisements.

7
Dishonesty never pays

During a casual talk I had with one of our managers, he asked me a very pertinent question, "Sir, in your opinion, what is the most important quality that a manager should have, to be successful in team-building?" Although the question took me by surprise, my response was immediate. "I strongly believe that the first quality that any manager needs in the process of team building is honesty and integrity. Your subordinates must feel that you have a high degree of integrity to the organization, and that you are honest with those who interact with you, both subordinates and superiors. They must feel from experience that you are trustworthy and dependable. People with honesty and integrity will always be successful in their lives; this is my studied view."

This reminds me of an old story. Once upon a time, there lived two brothers, who earned their livelihood by cutting fire-wood. The younger one was very straightforward and honest but the elder one

> Honesty and integrity build self esteem and confidence, which, in turn, win us the respect of others.

Dishonesty never pays

was greedy and crooked. One day, while cutting wood near the river bank, the younger one's axe slipped from his hands and fell into the river. He was very sad because he knew no work other than wood cutting, and did not have a spare axe with him. Suddenly, the River Goddess appeared before him and asked him about his grievance. With tears in his eyes, he narrated his problem. She disappeared beneath the water and returned with a golden axe and then asked him whether that was the one he had lost. The woodcutter replied that it was not his. She disappeared again and returned with a silver axe, but the woodcutter said that this too, did not belong to him. When she returned the third time with his iron axe, the woodcutter was delighted to get it back. In appreciation of his honesty, the Goddess gifted all the three axes to him.

The elder brother heard of this incident. He too wanted to get what his brother received. He went to the riverside and began chopping wood. But the axe never slipped away from his hands. When he was exhausted, he simply threw it into the river. When the Goddess appeared with a golden axe, the greedy woodcutter exclaimed, "Yes, this is mine, this is the one I lost!". The Goddess said that she would return with more golden axes and disappeared into the river. She never reappeared. The moral of the story is: "Dishonesty never pays".

If we are dishonest, we will never be trusted and we cannot build good interpersonal relationships. This applies to our professional, personal, and social lives as well. There may only be short-term gains. Honesty and integrity build selfesteem and confidence, which, in turn, win us the respect of others. You need to touch people's hearts to get the best out of them. They will do wonders if they are really motivated. This explains why, although some managers are smart and intelligent, they lack the support of their subordinates. At the same time, the honesty and integrity of those who may be relatively less capable, will enable them to produce better results, through a more effective delegation of work.

8
Give and Take

It is honesty and integrity, rather than smartness and intelligence, which are the key factors essential to become a good leader or a manager. I have always believed that any one who wants to come up in life, should follow the maxim, 'give respect and take respect', in his interactions with others. This 'give and take' policy is very essential to maintain harmony in an organization. If you are suspicious of your superiors, and maintain a disrespectful attitude towards them, it will impede your career growth in the organization, even if you are intelligent and smart.

> It is honesty and integrity, rather than smartness and intelligence, which are the key factors essential to become a good leader or a manager.

GIVE AND TAKE

This reminds me of the story of a Maharishi and his disciples. He was a scholar who could even predict the future through his meditation, and was able to read people's minds. He had a number of disciples. One of them was smart but not straightforward. He had come to the Maharishi only to study his special powers but had no respect for him. This disciple wanted to test the guru's 'Siddhi'.

One day he approached his guru, with a live butterfly hidden in his closed palms and asked, 'Sir, you are a man who can predict many things. Please tell me whether the butterfly that I hold in my palms, is alive or dead. The cunning disciple's intention was to squeeze the butterfly and kill it, if the guru said that it was alive, and to allow it to fly away, if he said that it was dead. In this way, he could defeat his guru, regardless of the answer he gave. But the Maharishi knew what the young fellow had in mind. He said, "The future of this butterfly depends entirely on your action, that is all". Thus he outwitted his cunning disciple.

In many cases you need not be a Maharishi to understand the true intentions of others, especially when you have opportunities to interact with them regularly. Manipulative people believe that they are smart, and that others are fools. They are reluctant to obey and respect their superiors. I have some advice for young managers and executives. Unless you sincerely respect and love your superiors, you can't earn the respect and love of your subordinates. They are watching your actions closely, and are most likely to copy your conduct and behaviour in day-to-day life. When we study ancient Indian culture, we see that the relationship between 'Guru & Shishya', was strongly built upon the principle: 'Give respect and earn respect'.

9
Positive Attitude Matters

We often come across people who always worry about trivial matters, and some others who tend to worry for no specific reason. When we interact with such people, they always talk about disasters and failures, and have a pessimistic approach, even towards good things. They keep moaning that life was much better in the old days and believe that the future will not be bright. In my childhood, I knew an elderly person who kept saying that the British rule was far better for India and that independence and democracy have ruined the country. Quoting the Bible, he would say that the changes we were seeing in

> It is mainly the force of negative thinking that retards progress.

the country, were an indication that the world would soon come to an end from a huge natural calamity, and so on. One important point that I want to add here, is that this person was a failure in his life, and I strongly believe that it was mainly due to his negative attitude. Some people have developed a habit of thinking negatively.

This reminds me of the story of a man who lived on the banks of a river which was very wide and deep, and always full of water. On the other side of the river, there was a dog that was properly chained up. Seated on this side of the river, the man thought, "If the river becomes dry and the dog is unleashed, what would be my fate?". When we hear this, we feel that it is foolish of him to entertain such thoughts, and that he is worrying for no reason. The probability of these two events occurring simultaneously, ie. the river becoming dry and the dog getting unleashed, is nil, and yet this man is worried! The moral of the story is that worry or anxiety, is purely a personal attitude towards an issue or problem. Regardless of the gravity of a situation, different people react differently, and many of them have negative attitudes.

When we analyze the lives of successful people, we see that the ability to remain calm and courageous in critical situations, is predominant in them, and that they remain composed even when disaster strikes. Only those who think positively, achieve higher and higher targets. It goes without saying, that decision-making will be delayed if one has fear of failure. History testifies that only those who accept challenges can conquer the world.

10
As our thoughts change, our lives change

Research has shown that on an average, a person generates about six hundred thoughts a day. It also reveals that about ninety percent of them are the same thoughts that we had the previous day. People who tend to have more negative thoughts than positive ones are called pessimists, while those who have more positive thoughts are called optimists. Our habits and character are all controlled by our own thoughts, which have a major role in determining our destiny. There is a well-known Malayalam proverb, "തലവര തലോടിയാൽ പോവില്ല", which means that we cannot change our destiny. But I strongly believe that we can change our destiny by changing our mind-set and our thought processes. If we can control our thoughts, we can control our minds, and if we can control our minds, we can control our lives.

> If we can control our thoughts, we can control our minds, and if we can control our minds, we can control our lives.

As our thoughts change, our lives change

In the animal kingdom, it is only human beings who have the special ability that helps them decide what to think and what not to think, in a given situation. This is why we have evolved as a species that is superior to all other animals. If we can train our minds to focus our thoughts positively, we can remain calm and composed even during disasters and in distress situations. We all know that the horse is one of the fastest and strongest animals in the world. When these animals are trained and disciplined, we derive immense benefit from their power and speed. At the same time, we know the devastation that can be caused by wild horses. Our thoughts gallop like horses. If we can rein them, we benefit personally, and mankind as a whole stands to gain. Otherwise, the outcome will be chaos. Remember, yogis and criminals are made out of the same flesh and bone. The only difference between them is in the orientation of their thought processes.

History shows that Indian maharishis recognized the importance of thought control, centuries ago. They knew that in order to have clear thoughts, one must have a cool mind, for which, we must first learn how to control our thoughts. If the water in a pond is still and clear, we can see our own image in it, whereas if it is dirty and turbulent, we cannot see anything.

We can apply the same principle to our minds as well. We must develop an attitude that there are no failures, only experiences and we must learn to see them in the right perspective, i.e. as opportunities to learn lessons which can serve as guidelines for later life. Failures are said to be "stepping stones to success."

11
A Rigid Mind Helps None

Somewhere I came across two highly thought provoking sentences. 'You cannot build a good team without good players. You can lose even with good players but you cannot win without them'. It is true that the attitudes of the team members are very important in determining the strength and success of the team. Inflexibility is one of the worst human traits. We can overcome fear with confidence, and laziness with discipline. But there is no remedy for the rigidity of one's mind. It carries the seeds of one's own destruction. There is a saying: 'Blessed are the flexible, for they shall not break'. People who are willing to change will always be successful in their endeavours.

> Rigidity of mind carries the seeds of one's own destruction

A Rigid Mind Helps None

Challenges have never been a problem to those who are adequately adaptable. They will find a solution for everything, even in very difficult situations. Flexibility and creativity go hand in hand. Adaptable people always place a high priority on breaking new grounds and attaining new targets. They realize that people are of varying abilities and temperaments. They have the special ability to accommodate all types of people. When we analyze the character traits of individuals who always succeed and flourish, we find that they are ever willing to change and rise to the occasion.

Another characteristic of adaptable people is their emotional stability. People who are not emotionally stable see everything as a threat or a danger. They may even become suspicious when a new talented person is introduced into the team, which may cause them to feel insecure in their position. A person's adaptability can be determined by the degree of pain he or she experiences on facing new situations. Creativity is another quality we find in adaptable people. When difficult situations arise, they are able to find alternative means to solve them, which leads to a new invention or discovery. In this way, adaptability fosters creativity.

Remember, the first quality required of a team player, is the willingness to fit into the team, and not to expect the team to adapt to his/her way. We come across people who are well accepted by others, and are also highly adaptable and emotionally stable. They will be successful in their personal, professional and social lives. It is because they possess these important traits that we call them leaders.

12

Strength in Unity

It is a known fact that working together harmoniously as a team, will definitely increase the efficiency which will eventually lead to success. Great challenges require good teamwork. The strength of a team chiefly depends on the cooperative mentality of the teammates in difficult situations. We can see some talented and capable people who prefer to work independently, in isolation, ignoring the fact that they are part of a team. Such people are found to entertain the false notion that only they are capable, and that others are incompetent. During my 29 years of experience in business, I have come across many such people, who perform well as individuals but fail miserably

> If we trust our people, we will treat them better and if we treat them better, they will do their best.

Strength in Unity

when they work in a team. They keep their cards close to their chest, and do not share ideas with others, because they want to appropriate full credit for the success.

All people have hopes, goals and dreams and would like to achieve success. There are some who are suspicious of their teammates, and a few others who are so pre-occupied with looking out for their own personal gains. They always use the word "I", rather than "we". If we trust our people, we will treat them better and if we treat them better, they will do their best. Sometimes their loyalty will be so deep rooted that they may even be prepared to sacrifice their lives for the organization.

This reminds me of a story about a few teenagers who were hiking through an estate where there was an abandoned rail track passing through the trees and leading to a demolished godown. One of the boys got onto the rail and tried walking on it. When he had taken but a few steps, he lost his balance. Another boy tried to do the same but he also failed, and the others laughed. He then challenged the others, 'I bet no one can do this, or prove otherwise'. One by one they tried, but all of them failed miserably. Even the best athlete and acrobat among them could not go more than a dozen steps without falling.

Two of the boys whispered to each other and came up with a plan. They declared to the others, 'The two of us can walk together on the rails all the way to the end'. On hearing this, those who had failed in the attempt, counter- challenged them, 'If you succeed, each of you will get a candy bar'. The two boys hopped up onto each rail, side by side, stretched out their arms, locked hands with each other and carefully walked the whole distance, and won the bet. The moral of the story is that, as individuals we cannot meet great challenges, but working together harmoniously we can easily accomplish big tasks with least effort. The combined strength of co-operation surpasses one's imagination. "United we stand, divided we fall".

13
The Power of Motivation

Throughout history, we find that all great leaders have been great motivators. We read in the great epic, the Mahabharat, that Bhagavan Sri Krishna's greatest contribution was to motivate Arjuna to fight against evil. In fact, the Bhagavad Gita, which contains his moving exhortation to Arjuna, has many elements of motivation in it. Similarly, Christ lived and died true to his principles and naturally he acquired a large following. The unassuming Mohandas Karamchand Gandhi mobilized the masses during the Independence movement and made history by being able to motivate them, setting his own life as an example. At one point he said, 'My life is my message'.

> Set yourself as an example and motivate people

The Power of Motivation

I strongly believe that a mere academic title or degree from one of the premier management institutions, such as Harvard or IIM will not create a great manager or leader. It is only when others around you feel that you are honest, trustworthy, dependable and capable that they will hold you in high regard and be willing to cooperate with you and assist you, With very few exceptions, the vast majority of people prefer to be guided, and they seek real leaders. The success of a leader depends entirely on the way he or she motivates the subordinates. Gone are the days when people could be compelled to do things under an autocratic or authoritarian dictate.

This reminds me of the story of a cap seller. He used to earn his livelihood by selling caps in the village, carrying them around in a large gunny bag, slung over his shoulder. When he walked a long distance, he felt tired and decided to rest for a while under a tree. He sat there, with the bag kept open to display the caps for sale, but soon fell asleep as he was thoroughly exhausted. When he woke up a few minutes later, he was shocked to find that his bag was empty, and he was left with only the cap he wore on his head. The man looked up and saw some monkeys on the tree with the hats on their heads. Out of frustration, he began shouting and making gestures at them. Immediately, the monkeys responded by screeching back at him and making the same gestures.

In desperation, he removed the cap from his head. Suddenly all the monkeys removed the caps from their heads. He watched the instinct of imitation so strong in them. He said to himself "I can get back my caps only by motivating them". In a vehement gesture, he threw his cap at the monkeys. As expected, all the monkeys imitated him and threw the caps back at him. Thus, he recovered all his caps and went away. You cannot get things done the way you want, by shouting at others. The only solution is to set yourself as an example and motivate people.

14

Don't underestimate anyone

Building a strong team is as important as producing a quality product or venturing into a big project. The vision of the organization must be, to allow the best ideas to rise from the bottom of the ladder to the top, and to have them implemented. The various Heads of Departments have a major role in motivating their subordinates to come up with the best suggestions and must see that these are put into practice. However, this can happen only if we have good faith and confidence in our subordinates.

When V-Guard was in its infancy, it was a one-man show, of an entrepreneur with just two workers. Much has happened since then,

Do not underestimate the work done by others

Don't underestimate anyone

and today we can proudly proclaim that the strength of V-Guard is its teamwork. I have strong faith and confidence in my subordinates, and I wish that all managers in the various departments possessed the same attitude. But there is no use being blind to reality. Some managers just cannot trust their subordinates. They claim that they are doing it to protect the interests of the organization. But let me ask them, "Don't you think I have the same concern? If I were like you, and thought like you, you wouldn't be in our team!"

Some managers tend to believe that their own department ranks high in terms of its importance and efficiency, whereas all other departments in the organization serve no useful purpose. This reminds me of an incident, said to have happened on board a ship where the captain and the chief engineer would constantly argue about the importance of their work. Each of them claimed that his expertise was the most crucial factor in the running of the ship. The debate got more and more heated and finally they decided that they would exchange jobs for a day. The chief engineer would be on the bridge and navigate the ship, while the captain would go down to the engine room.

Only a few hours into their shift, the captain emerged from the engine room sweating, his face and uniform covered with grease and oil. "Chief, the engine has come to a grinding halt. I have tried my best but haven't been able to set things right. You need to get down to the engine room. I can't get her go". The desperate chief engineer replied, "I was about to call you, I made a mistake in navigation; we have lost our way and the ship has landed on a sand bed!" Each of them had gone wrong in estimating the importance of the work done by the other. Pay due respect to the work done by others in their own departments. Do not underestimate the work done by another person. Individually one may be smart, but a team is smarter.

15

Self-Transformation furthers Development

The strength of a chain is determined at its weakest link. Regardless of the strength of the other links, the weakness of just one can make it unable to pass the load test. One need not be a mechanical engineer to understand this simple fact. This applies to every process in the functioning of an organisation. The more the number of weak links that you find in an organization, by which I am referring to those middle level managers who perform below par, the more retarded its growth will be. A healthy organization has to grow fast. In this era of globalization and liberalization, the growth must be fast enough to keep up with the pace of a fast chaging world, lest the enterprise should become decadent and eventually be outmoded.

> Self-transformation can happen only when one looks within oneself

Self-Transformation furthers Development

'The weak links', ie., those middle level managers who under-perform, are the curse of any growing organisation. Some tend to believe that promotions are a natural process within an organization, whereby after a few years, they get promoted automatically. Here comes the importance of self- development. One may be very sincere, hardworking, trustworthy and proficient in one's subject, but if one's critical managerial abilities such as communication skills, emotional intelligence and general knowledge are poor, one cannot move up the ladder. I strongly believe that self-development must be a continuous process, and it is something for which I devote considerable time, even at age 60. The acquisition of new skills and knowledge must be a part of our life.

As an individual, self-transformation can happen only when one looks within oneself with a willingness to grow and extend further beyond oneself. A leader must be ambitious and must have an urge to overcome one's own weaknesses. To become efficient managers, there are five essential guidelines to be followed:

1. Motivate other team members
2. Be ready to grab responsibility
3. Strive to overcome personal weaknesses
4. Cultivate a 'Think Big' attitude
5. Persevere to justify the overall expectations of the department.

The most important of these is the third one; 'Strive to overcome personal weaknesses'. If one succeeds in doing that, all other skills will follow suit. The law of nature is: 'You cannot grow beyond your ambitions'. If there is a will, there is a way. If you have no ambition and are not willing to work to overcome your personal weaknesses, no one else can help you!. 'A striving sinner is better than a contented saint.'

16

The 4 C's of Effective Communication

If we want to run an organization like a smooth, well-oiled machine, effective communicative skill is an important ingredient which we cannot afford to ignore. When you apply grease or lubricant at junctional points, the performance of a machine will be more efficient, and it will function smoothly. Similarly, group dynamics is the essence of the success of any organization and communication plays a vital role as a lubricant. If communication is poor, the co-workers will be unsure of their tasks, which, in turn, is bound to tell upon their performance. They have a right to know why they were told to do a given task, in a particular manner. If you have ever been in a team where the teammates didnot let one another know what was going on, then you must surely have experienced its baneful impact upon your own performance. Uninhibited communication increases co-operation and commitment, which, in turn, fuels action. If we expect employees to trust their leaders, effective communication is the only means to gain it. The communication must be unequivocal and unambiguous and should convey all the required information. You must have patience

> Clarity, Consistency, Courtesy and Concern form the essence of effective communication.

The 4 C's of Effective Communication

and devote enough time to explain things in detail. If you wish to communicate with nursery class students effectively, you must first go down to their level, and speak slowly in their baby language. Only then will they respond to you and be attentive enough to understand you. The same is true with your team members. To convince them, you have to talk in their language in sufficient detail. I believe that a 4C formula, comprising Clarity, Consistency, courtesy and Concern, is applicable to effective communication.

1. Clarity: A team cannot perform effectively if the members do not know what you expect of them. Clarity in explanations is vital. What is the purpose of the task? Why have you asked them to do it in a particular way? Generally, people at the higher levels in the organization are less descriptive in their instructions, and are least bothered with giving details. At the same time, people at lower levels are eager to get detailed instructions on what has to be done.

2. Consistency: First of all, leaders must make up their minds on what to do, and what not to do. If ideas keep changing constantly, it will confuse and frustrate the other team members. A team leader's hasty actions, which are carried out at the last minute, without doing proper homework and planning, cause the worst hindrance to teamwork.

3. Courtesy: A leader can create a friendly atmosphere in the organization by being courteous, and this kind of positive behaviour is, in fact, contagious. Everyone deserves to be respected, no matter what his/her rank or position be.

4. Concern: An effective leader must be concerned about the welfare of his teammates. They must feel safe and comfortable under his leadership. If you are concerned about your teammates, just as you are concerned about your children, then they will go to any length to support your initiatives. If you can apply this 4C formula in your communications, then you will be a popular and people-oriented manager.

17

People Management

A journalist once asked me, "You have always been acknowledged as a people-oriented leader. To what extent have your values and ethics helped you gain the reputation? What are the philosophies and principles in your life?" I managed to give him a satisfactory reply, although it was not well planned. Later on, I introspected and tried to identify the guiding forces that have helped me to become a people-oriented person. I understand that people recognize us by our achievements and character, rather than the clothes, watch or shoes we wear. A detailed analysis reveals four major qualities that are required to make one a people-oriented leader.

> People recognize us by our achievements and character

1. Give respect and take respect: No matter what position a person holds, everyone expects to be treated with dignity and respect. Even a starving person values his or her ego more than food. Respect is subjective and is reflected in one's readiness to accept human dignity. We must always keep our eyes and ears open and be polite. Respect is not a one way street. Unless we treat others with respect, we cannot expect the same from them.
2. Be fair and firm: We must be fair in our dealings, even if we incur some loss in certain situations. It is easy to keep our word if everything goes well. The real litmus test of fairness, is our reaction at the time of a crisis. It is always good to engage in frequent introspection, where we ask ourselves, 'Is it fair to all concerned?' Once you are fair, you have every right to be firm. In many situations, one must be firm, otherwise people will exploit you. One can disagree without being disagreeable.
3. Create less inconvenience for your co-passengers: Everyone uses up a certain amount of space in this beautiful world. We should not expand our territory at the cost of others. A win-win attitude is an ideal strategy for a people-oriented leader. A 'Live and let live' policy will bring harmony not only in organizations but also in society, as a whole. If the various religious and political leaders in our country had strictly followed this principle, India would have become a heaven on earth by now.
4. Be punctual and organized: To be a popular manager, one must be time conscious. The public will find it difficult to deal with someone who is not at all punctual and systematic. Remember, your subordinate's time is also precious, and they may have their own personal problems and priorities. Time consciousness makes one easily acceptable to others. To put it in a nutshell, a leader stands on the top of a human pyramid and the height of the pyramid is directly proportional to the strength and width of the base. If human relations are weak, no leader can attain higher and higher targets.

18

Strong values build strong Teams

Mother Teresa once said, "You can do what I cannot do. I can do what you cannot do. Together we can do great things." This simple message conveys the real meaning of the power of teamwork. It is admitted by everyone that there are lots of advantages in teamwork. But to get the best out of teamwork, team members have to pool their resourcefulness in harmony for the betterment of the organization. The real glue that helps the team members to stick together is the values and ethics upheld by the organization. Values can help a team to become more synthesised and productive. Just as personal values influence and guide the behavior of an individual, organizational values influence and guide the team's cohesion and output.

Values can help a team to become more synthesised and more productive.

There is a saying 'Birds of the same feather flock together'. Similarly, a group of like-minded people can get along very easily and work together in synergy. If we are trying to build up a relationship with someone, we begin to search for the things the other person has in common with us. That means we need something to build on, and common values make the strongest base. Values also help to set the standards for the performance of the team. These are often expressed in a mission statement, as a set of guidelines for doing business. But sometimes, the stated values of an organization and the values they practise, do not match, and people can easily notice the difference. My studied view is that the difference between what you preach and what you practise, should be brought down to the bare minimum.

I strongly believe in the precept that, 'the moment you give up your values and ethics, you lose your identity'. When individuals possess strong values, they help them to make correct decisions. The same principle is applicable to organizations also. If the team members have strong values and ethics, the organization will grow steadily because of correct decision making. In my thirty years of experience in business, the most valuable lesson that I have learned is that, "There is no short cut to long term success".

If the organization cannot inculcate time-tested values and principles into its staff members, real growth will ever remain elusive. Any ambitious individual has to focus on leadership development. The potential already exists within us, and if we feed it with values and ethics, the power of the individual will scale great heights. I believe 'Everything rises and falls on leadership, and values and principles have a lot to do with long term success'.

19
Leadership Success

One of my classmates at college, who is now a retired government servant, once asked me, "We are both of the same age, and yet you continue to be active in your business, which, owing to your zeal and vigour, is ever expanding. What is the motivation behind this?" I replied that the day we stop growing, marks the start of our decline.

Some people believe that if they have been able to achieve a particular goal, they can rest contented for the rest of their life. This can happen when we pursue any goal, such as earning a degree, securing a coveted position, receiving a particular award or achieving

A leader should come out of his comfort zone, take risks and try to break new grounds.

a financial target. True leaders cannot afford to think that way. A leader should come out of his comfort zone, take risks and try to break new grounds.

One has to pay a high price to become a champion. Remaining on top will cost even more, and improving upon your best is still more expensive. The higher up you go, the more you have to struggle to progress further. Olympic champion sprinters improve upon their timings not by seconds, but by milliseconds! Remember there is no victory at bargain prices.

It is a universal law that when you give your best to the world, the whole world will honor you and will give you the best in return. Similarly, a team will reach the pinnacle of its potential only if its leader reaches the top of his/her best performance. That is the nature of the responsibility a leader has, and there is no escaping it.

I have ample reason to believe that organizations and brands are living entities. We have to inject life and energy into them on a continuous basis, lest they tend to decay. In any growing organization, an effective manager will delegate his present responsibilities to his immediate juniors, and take up new challenges. For that, we must train our juniors to take up new responsibilities.

The secret of success in a relay race, mainly depends on two things: How smoothly one person hands over the baton to the next one, and how fast each person can run until the last one in the series touches the finishing point. The growth of an organization is similar to the relay race in many ways.

20
Keep an Open Mind

The growth of any organisation is dependent to a great extent on the innovations taking place in its departments. We need to generate new ideas on a continuous basis, in order to achieve diverse objectives, such as reducing the cost of production, delivering better after sales service and, evolving a dependable marketing strategy. To compete effectively in this globalised economy, we have to think out of the box. If we analyze the functioning of successful and fast growing organizations, we are sure to find that their trump card is the innovations that take place in all their departments, which helps them to retain the edge.

If we think that we know everything, then we cannot improve ourselves.

Keep an Open Mind

I am convinced that any human being of average intelligence and experience, can generate new ideas. He or she need not be a first rank holder or a genius to come up with innovative ideas. The most important thing is that we must believe that there is always room for improvement, in the way we do things now. We must also be willing to try new methods and be ready to face some initial setbacks. Inquisitiveness is one major quality, which is essential to be innovative. We must have the mindset of a school student, with a willingness to learn more.

In this context, I am reminded of the story of a proud professor, who decided to learn Philosophy and approached a very learned Buddhist monk. Instead of learning in all humility the professor began boasting of his achievements and knowledge to the monk, who soon became fed up with his attitude. One day while the monk was teaching him the finer details of Philosophy, the professor interrupted him frequently and tried to demonstrate his knowledge of the subject. At this point, the monk asked his servant to bring a kettle of tea and a teacup. When they were brought, the monk began pouring tea from the kettle into the cup. He continued to pour, even after the cup was full. It soon overflowed and the tea spilt onto the table. Irritated with this, the professor shouted 'Stop! Can't you see the cup is full?' The monk calmly replied with a smile, 'And so is your mind. Unless you empty it, how can you learn? Just as it is not possible for me to pour any more tea into this teacup which is already full, I cannot impart any more wisdom to you, because your mind is swollen with too much conceit that it cannot imbibe anything."

If we think that we know everything, then we cannot improve ourselves. If we think that our present activities are perfect in every way, we cannot think about changes. But if we have the mindset to change and are willing to take a closer look at the way we do things, we will certainly notice that there is a lot of room for change. And it is this realization that triggers creativity, and leads to innovations.

21
Hard Work Pays

During an interaction with a group of MBA students, one of them raised an interesting question, 'What is the most important quality one must possess to be successful in life?' I replied that there are many qualities required to become a successful person, and all of them are important. In my view, there are at least twenty or twenty-five different yet vital factors that are required to make a person successful in life. Of these, the ability to 'stretch one's limits' is what I choose to elaborate in some detail.

If we have the inclination and the willingness to work hard, we can stretch our limits to any extent.

Hard Work Pays

All human beings have a lot of inherent potential within them. It is our duty to identify those talents, polish them, and bring them out to light. This process of polishing needs to be a continuous exercise. Unless we stretch ourselves to the limit, we cannot excel in our profession. History reveals that success is guaranteed to those who are ambitious and ready to work hard with persistence and consistence.

This reminds me of the story of a village youth, who was fond of physical exercise and body- building. As there was no gymnasium in his village, he used to practise by lifting heavy stones and wooden logs of various sizes. One day, a cow in his household, delivered a cute and beautiful calf. Thereafter, the young man added one more item to his routine exercise; he began to lift the calf ten times a day, and practised this on a regular basis.

Months and years went by, and our youngster zealously continued his routine exercise. By now, three to four years had already gone by, and although the calf had become a full-grown ox, the young man could lift it effortlessly. He was able to do this only because of his persistent effort on a long-term basis. He never noticed that he had been adding 100 to 200 grams everyday to his weightlifting load.

If we have the inclination and the willingness to work hard, we can stretch our limits to any extent. Remember, success is not a clear-cut destination, but a never-ending journey. Success after success is called for, before a person can rise to the stature of a leader. If we decide to march forward rapidly with proper planning, we can overcome any number of obstacles. In this task we need only one thing - a firm resolve. If there is a will, there is a way.

22
Flexibility in decision making

I happened to read a research paper, which pointed out that nine out of ten start-up companies perish within ten years! This is the global average and the failure rates are much higher in developing countries like India. It also reveals that rarely do we find instances of a small scale industry successfully evolving into a medium scale enterprise, and eventually attaining the status of a large business corporate. I believe that the compatible teamwork that exists in an organization is the main reason for its growth. The flexibility of a company's managers is

The flexibility of a Company's managers is the lubricant that facilitates its smooth functioning.

Flexibility in Decision Making

the lubricant that facilitates its smooth functioning. If a manager is very rigid and egoistic, with an authoritarian attitude, the performance of the team that he leads will decline sharply. In any organization we come across a few people who are very stubborn and rigid. In my opinion, such rigidity can ultimately end up in one's own ruin.

From time immemorial, the tribals of Africa have known how to trap monkeys quite easily. They select a small pot with an opening, just enough for a monkey's paw to slip through. A few nuts are placed in the pot, which is then tied to the branch of a tree. Attracted by the smell of the nuts, monkeys collect at the place. Having reached at the nuts, the monkey instinctively clenches its fist to keep the nuts sure and secure. However much it may try, it cannot extricate its paw, tightened as it is. Come what may, a monkey will not loosen its fist. Then the inevitable happens. Lots of monkeys are captured in this way.

If only they had let go of the nuts! But their inherant nature is to stick to the same decision till the end, and this leads to their own ruin. They are unwilling to change their minds to meet the needs of a new situation and are inflexible in decision-making.

In Malayalam literature, those who are very stubborn in character, are described by the term, 'markadamushti,' meaning 'monkey's fist'. All these show that rigidity in decision making leads to negative results. I strongly believe that the greatest asset of a leader is to have a high degree of flexibility and adaptability.

23
Learn to Lead

I strongly believe that there are no born leaders. To lead is a skill like any other, that is acquired with hard work and practice. In time, it becomes part of your personality and that is why sometimes people think that leadership is predisposed.

Let me elaborate this point. I was only a mediocre student during my school and college days, and my grades were just average. I was basically a shy person, with poor communicative ability. Since I was born and brought up in a remote village, my exposure to sophisticated social life was very limited, and it was very difficult for me to write and speak in English. Moreover, I have a learning disability called dyslexia, a reading and writing disorder, where numbers and words appear to me in a disorganized manner. During my younger days, my emotional maturity level was

> Whatever managerial skills I have today, are all acquired ones. Success is earned, not got.

low, and I had a weak memory. Furthermore, public speaking was a nightmare for me. I still remember the day when I delivered my first public speech, before a small gathering, when my legs were literally shivering. With all these handicaps, how can I be termed a born leader?

My only predominant positive trait, was a good aptitude for science subjects, especially physics, and my ambition was to become a scientist in a leading research organization such as ISRO, BARC or any other reputed entity. But I could not secure such a coveted position, and was finally forced to start a small-scale industry of my own. Initially, it was virtually a one-man show, and I had to involve myself literally in every facet of the business, including marketing, finance, taxation and production. After a few years I realized that technical abilities alone would not help me to run the establishment successfully.

It then dawned on me that I had to train myself to overcome my weaknesses, so I began attending various types of personality development programs. I also developed a habit of reading books on management, which helped me a lot in later years. If you ask me how many training programs I have attended and how many books I have read, my answer would be quite a lot. Since I spent a great deal of time attending these programs, I would often come home late. Both my sons were small kids in those days, and my wife had a tough time managing them on her own. She once expressed her concern openly, "My brothers also are engaged in business but they do not attend such management training sessions. What is so special in your case?". I replied, "I know my weaknesses, and I have to overcome them and improve myself. That is all." Now, all those laborious years spent in attending those programmes with a genuine zeal to learn have born fruit. The effort was worth it. I am now quite conivinced from my own experience that leadership skills are cultivated over time and one has to work towards it.

24

Commonsense is quite uncommon

A businessman once purchased a specially gifted parrot from a pet shop. The shopkeeper told him that this parrot could speak three different languages; Hindi, English and Tamil. The demonstration that followed showed that he was right, that it could successfully repeat his words in these three languages. He paid a hefty sum and bought the parrot with great enthusiasm.

Since he was on his way to his office, the businessman engaged a porter to deliver the parrot and its cage in his house. He rushed home

> During crisis situations, the ability to correctly analyze the pros and cons of the issue at hand, and take the right decision, is the 'litmus test' of a successful person.

Commonsense is quite uncommon

in the afternoon greatly excited, and asked his wife about the parrot. The wife replied, 'Just this morning, I read a special recipe for fried parrot, and it was sheer coincidence that you sent the parrot on the same day. You can have this special delicacy for dinner; it has already been cooked.' This came as a great shock to him, and he exclaimed, 'This was a costly parrot which could speak three different languages; Hindi, English and Tamil.' The wife replied, 'In that case, it could have pleaded in any of the three languages, `Don't kill me!', but I could hear only screeching sounds.'

The pertinent point here, is that whatever we learn, has to be put into practice in our day-to-day lives; otherwise, it can lead to pernicious consequences. When the need arose, the parrot did not utilize the knowledge it had acquired. We sometimes come across such people amongst us. Years ago, with great expectations, we appointed an experienced person with an MBA degree, as one of our distributors. Within six months, we realized that he was very poor in business administration, although he had a master's degree in the subject. Eventually, we were compelled to discontinue his distributorship.

Here comes the importance of practical wisdom and common sense. There is a saying that 'Common sense is quite uncommon'. The ability to make a decision promptly is essential for success in life. The right decision should be taken at the right time. During crisis situations, the ability to correctly analyze the pros and cons of the issue at hand, and take the right decision, is crucial.

25

Delegation paves the way to success

When a journalist asked me about my vision and plan for the next five years, I had no hesitation to say that I would play the role of a motivator. I added, 'I am already 57 years old, and in the V-Guard group, we have many talented, experienced managers and officers at different levels. If I can motivate and guide them, the output will be immense.' I always believe that there are limits for an individual to excel, whereas, if you have a group of people with a proper leader, then the team's performance will be stupendous.

> There must be trust, respect, commitment and faith in relationships and only then can an organization put up its best.

I now prefer to sit in the seat adjacent to that of the driver. I prefer to allow others to drive. This task is more challenging than driving oneself. First of all, one must have faith in the capabilities of others. For that matter, I have enough confidence to entrust responsibilities to others. We often come across people who, while occupying the seat adjacent to the driver, go on directing him and giving minute instructions, even to a well experienced one. Very often they get so deeply involved, that they will inadvertently press their right foot firmly on the floor, as if they are applying the brakes! Incessant interruptions and undue involvement can do more harm than good.

There must be an emotional bond between the leader and his subordinates. The trainer must have full faith in the trainees. If the leader has no confidence in his subordinates or if the subordinates have no faith in the leader, then the organization will be weak and inefficient. There must be trust, respect, commitment and faith in relationships and only then, can an organization put up its best. Here, the leader must create a motivated environment, so that the enthusiasm among the team members will get boosted.

Many organizations fizzle out at the death of their founder, while many other great organizations will far outlive their founders. To make that possible, the founder has to provide well in advance such an atmosphere and a system within the organization, that even in his absence it will run smoothly. My vision is that, even in my absence, the organization should not feel a vacuum. Empowering subordinates to take up new challenges is, in my view, the only method that can realize this vision.

26

Introspection Leads to Success

During a training program, the lecturer asked his audience, "Who is your competitor?'. Many people began to talk about the competition they faced in the real world like the marketing arena. A few among them pointed to the unethical methods, adopted by some of their local competitors. But the trainer took them by surprise when he said, "Your only real competitor is you yourself!". This reply raised many eyebrows and the audience could not guess what he meant by the embarrassing statement.

He expatiated on the subject. From his explanation, it became clear that the main stumbling blocks for personal growth, are a

> Very few people choose to correct themselves and those who do so, are bound to be successful in life.

Introspection Leads to Success

lack of commitment, integrity, industry, confidence, and such other factors. When we study the story of the success of any organization, we find behind it a team of efficient people with efficient systems. This is applicable not only to commercial organizations but also to political parties, religious congregations and so on. Socialism in Russia collapsed, not because of any external interference, but on account of the deterioration in principles and discipline within the Communist party itself. It was the natural downfall of a political system from its own inherent weakness.

This applies to individuals even more. Our personal growth is directly proportionate to our attitude. It is not so easy for anyone to conduct a self-analysis of one's own deficiencies. On the other hand, others can easily recognize our mistakes. Our most intimate friends will be reluctant to disclose to us, what exactly we lack in our character. So the first step, for those who want to develop themselves and be successful, should be to make frequent self introspection and try to find out one's own shortcomings. When there is a setback, our natural tendency is to find fault with others, with a pre-disposition that we can never go wrong. This attitude will be highly detrimental to progress in our career and in life as a whole.

There is a saying; 'If you have a defect on your face, don't blame the mirror.' Everybody knows that it is sheer foolishness to break the mirror for a blemish on one's countenance. But in our day-to-day lives, we always find fault with others when in fact, the problem lies with us. Everyone tends to think that he is infallible, and that others are responsible for all his problems. It is easy to criticize others. Most people have the attitude of 'I am OK, You are not OK". Very few people choose to correct themselves and those who do so, are bound to be successful in life.

27

Empowerment

A customer at a restaurant once asked the waiter, 'What time is it?', and the latter replied, 'Sorry, that is not my table'. Now you can imagine what type of service we would get in this restaurant. Everyone knows that if you treat your customers well, they will return to buy from you. It is very clear that the waiter's response would have had just the opposite effect.

In another incident, a reporter, who was also the photographer of a newspaper, went to report on a tennis match, which was to be held in an indoor stadium, but returned promptly to the press office. When the editor asked him for the report, he replied, 'There was

> Employees must be empowered to take decisions at their levels, and should not have to constantly go to their boss or supervisor for approval.

no tournament today'. 'What happened?', asked the editor. 'There was a big fire and the whole stadium collapsed', replied the reporter. 'Then where is the photograph and the report of the fire?', the editor continued. 'That is not my duty. I am only a sports journalist!' said the reporter". It's anybody's guess if the reporter still had a job.

Although slightly exaggerated, in both cases the message is the same: the word 'service' has different dimensions. If we are in business, each staff member must be capable of dealing with any situation, without any preconceived notions. I cannot lay the blame entirely on the waiter or the reporter in these examples. Here, the management also had the responsibility to give clear instructions in advance, on how to deal with different situations. Employees must be empowered to take suitable decisions at their levels, and should not have to constantly go to their boss or supervisor for approval. An authoritative, 'Just do what I say' attitude of top management will serve but to create a set of inefficient employees in the organisation.

There is a saying 'There are no bad soldiers, only bad generals'. A war is lost, not because of the inefficiency of ordinary soldiers on foot in the front row, but because of the wrong tactics of the officers who give instructions from behind. There is no need to write down in minutest detail all the policies and procedures in the organization's manual. Instead, a culture has to be developed that empowers the employees becomingly. If the employees fully understand the company's philosophy in doing business, and receive good training therein, there is no need to elaborate on what needs to be done in every situation. The company must show trust and confidence that its employees will take appropriate decisions and actions in given situations. In turn, employees should live up to their expectations. The customers will love to deal with a company of smart leaders and quick decision makers, regardless of their rank. Eventually, the success of such companies is sure and certain.

28
Think before you leap

One essential quality that we find in great leaders, is that they all follow the golden rule, 'Think before you speak, and think before you act'. All of us have a weakness, that we react hastily without knowing all the relevant facts of an issue. This kind of reaction often triggers off a conflict. It is a well-known law of nature that friction will generate heat and too much heat will produce a spark, which often leads to an explosion. The same principle applies to human relations also. So, to maintain healthy human relationships, it is essential to 'analyze and know the facts before you act'.

> Analyze and know the facts before you act.

Think before you leap

This reminds me of the story of a woman in a village, who had an unusual pet – a mongoose. She had acquired it several years before, when it was only a baby, and had raised it like a pet dog in her house. This woman had a two-month old baby. One day while the baby was asleep, she went out to fetch water from the nearby river. Since there was no one at home, she entrusted the mongoose with the care of the sleeping child.

When she returned, she was shocked to see the mongoose in the veranda, stained with blood all over the body. She immediately thought that the mongoose had killed her baby. In a fit of anger, she picked up a big stone, threw it at the mongoose and killed it. She then went inside the room, where she saw the unexpected. A cobra that had just been killed, lay in a pool of blood, next to the infant, who was sleeping peacefully, unaware of everything that had happened. What a tragedy! The mongoose had, in fact, saved her baby at the dire risk of its own life.

The moral of the story is quite simple; never take a hasty decision without assessing all the facts of a given situation. On certain occasions, our subordinates may have tried their utmost to fulfill a particular task. But, for one reason or another, they may have failed to accomplish it. If we criticize, without analyzing the facts and knowing the real motive, our criticism would be, indeed, painful to them. No one likes to be blamed, if he/she have not been at fault. One should take the time to think and analyze the facts twice or even thrice, before making any remarks or taking decisions, regardless of whether it concerns an official or a personal matter. This will definitely improve our human relations. Otherwise, we may have to repent later.

29

Everything is not what it appears

Thoughtless remarks often spoil professional, social and even family relationships. There is a saying, 'The pen is mightier than the sword'. I would like to add, 'The tongue is sharper than the sword'. Even though it is made up of soft tissue, the tongue is a very sharp weapon. It is potent enough to kill the reputation of other people, which is more precious than life itself.

> In certain situations, we may easily get carried away and assume something which may not be true.

Everything is not what it appears

In many cases, family relationships are ruined because of gossip or hearsay. We may have some pre-conceived notions about people and situations. They will induce us to make comments or judgments without knowing the real facts.

This reminds me of the story of a youngster, who saved a child from being drowned in a swimming pool. One evening, a pool side party was being held in a hotel, where all the guests were in a jubilant mood, which was suddenly spoilt, when a small child fell into the deep end of the pool. Everyone was in panic and no one dared to jump in and save the drowning child. All of a sudden, to everyone's surprise, a well-dressed youngster jumped into the pool, still wearing his costly clothes and saved the child.

When the rescue operation was over, everyone began praising the youngster for his great courage. The child's father announced that the young man would receive a costly gift for his bravery. On receiving the appreciation and the gift the youngster asked a question which embarassed everyone, 'Who pushed me into the pool? I didn't have courage enough to jump into the pool!' The simple truth was that someone had pushed him in. Probably, he prized his expensive clothes more than the life of a stranger.

In this instance, the spectators drew their own conclusions based on what they believed to be true in those circumstances. But now we know that the truth was totally different. The point I would like to emphasize here is that, in certain situations, we can easily get carried away and assume something which may not be true. Numerous similar occasions may arise when we work as a team. We may often blame our subordinates for failing in their duty despite their best efforts, when in fact, there may have been unknown factors responsible for the adverse outcome. So, think twice or even thrice before you speak and act.

30
Seize every opportunity

Searching for new opportunities is one of the key factors of success. Opportunities constantly present themselves before us, and we need only to keep our eyes open, to spot them. Instances are many, when we leave golden chances unexploited, mistaking them to be of no relevance or value. But the truth can be quite different. The search for new avenues can be done meaningfully, only if we have an open mind and a positive outlook, and an indomitable urge for achieving new goals. Even in adverse conditions, there will be some hidden opportunities, but we need to really take a close look, to see them.

> We have to search for available Opportunities which are sometimes hidden, but within our reach

Seize every opportunity

This reminds me of the story of a South African farmer, who had extensive farmland in a rural area. His ambition was to become a billionaire. He believed that he would not be able to fulfill his desire by farming in a village. In fact, he made use of only a small part of his farmland and the lions share of it was lying uncultivated. He decided to sell his property in the village and move to the town, so that he could engage in business and fulfill his ambition to become a billionaire.

The man who bought this farmland thought, 'I will work hard on this land, and convert every inch of it into agricultural land, and earn my livelihood.' He started work on the very first day; he levelled the land and ploughed the land tirelessly. One day when ploughing, he noticed what looked like a few pieces of shining rock. A closer look convinced him that these were actually rough diamonds of high quality. A deeper study revealed that there were huge deposits of diamonds underneath his land. Eventually he became a billionaire!

The first landowner made the mistake of not exploiting opportunities already available to him. He never knew that he was sitting on a diamond mine! The second owner, unaware of the hidden treasure that lay below, worked hard and eventually struck gold. Some people may see an element of luck in it but, in my opinion, it was the hard work put in by the second owner, which brought him his fortune. Similarly, we have to search for available opportunities which lie hidden, but are within our reach.

As human beings we have a tendency to believe that 'The grass is greener on the other side of the fence.' Most often we fail to notice that the grass in our own yard is as green, if not greener than the other. There is no meaning in simply claiming that 'we have eyes'! We have to really keep them wide open and look for new avenues. If we are ready to change our attitude, success will be ours.

31

One's Fate lies in One's own Hands

In our day-to-day lives, we come across many people who always think negatively and are obsessed with the thought of failures, setbacks and disasters. They generally believe that no growth or development can happen in their own town or state, or even in the whole country. They can give countless reasons to substantiate their argument. Such people get easily agitated over trivial matters, and are generally victims of ill health. For no reason, their basically pessimistic temperament leads them to fear that death is imminent.

This reminds me of an incident which was reported in the newspapers. A well-experienced refrigerator mechanic was repairing a walk-in type of deep freezer which could stock tons of meat and fish,

> In every crisis situation, there will be a ray of hope, but we should be prepared and willing to search for it.

and withstand temperature up to minus 30ºC. He had rectified all the major defects and the freezer was ready to work. But unfortunately, the big door of the freezer closed automatically and he was trapped inside. As an experienced mechanic, he knew that when the door is shut, the freezer would start functioning and the cooling would begin automatically. No one could open the door from inside.

The man knew that the freezer had very thick doors, and even if he banged on them or made a loud noise, it would not be loud enough to draw anyone's attention, since the sound would not be heard outside. Being a pessimist, the man was convinced that his life would soon come to an end. He felt a chill in his body and the cold was getting so severe that he began shivering. He continued to feel unbearable cold and finally he died. A few minutes later, when the door was opened by some other staff members, they saw the mechanic's dead body.

To everyone's surprise, the main electrical supply was found to have been already disconnected from the freezer, which was, in fact, not working! So, although the temperature within was the same as that outside, the man had died! The post-mortem report revealed that death had occurred neither due to lack of oxygen, nor to freezing cold. In fact, he had died of fear, which affected his heart. Due to his negative mindset, the man did not even hope that someone would open the door from outside.

In every crisis situation, there will be a ray of hope, but we should be prepared and willing to search for it. A survey conducted among retail investors in the stock market revealed that those who tend to think negatively, lose more money out of fear, when the stocks dip. An analysis of the traits of leaders and successful people, will reveal that a positive outlook lies hidden in their character. Whatever success I have had in my life, has been mainly due to my unfailing optimistic outlook, and not the product of a high level of intelligence. In fact, I believe that I may not be as intelligent as many others, if a comparison is made.

32
The IPO Challenge

It was an uphill task for me to take V-Guard to the capital market in 2008, when it was really bearish and turbulent. Soon after we had fixed the issue opening dates, the IPO of two other reputed companies, failed in the market during their issue. Even many corporate giants were affected to the extent that their price was quoted below the issue price, after it was listed. Many reputed companies postponed their issues fearing a further dip in the stock market. The Sensex slumped to 16 thousand from the peak of 21 thousand.

Many knowledgeable people in this field advised me to postpone the date of our issue. But I chose to ignore it and to go ahead, because I had great confidence in the many lakhs of our satisfied customers and knew they would support us even during the worst market conditions.

'When the sky is the darkest, the stars shine the brightest'

The IPO Challenge

We had more than 1,400 committed employees in our group companies, who were willing to work hard to make the 'impossible' a reality. I was confident that the goodwill V-Guard had earned over three decades, would help us in this task. Our wide network of dealers and distributors must act as our brand ambassadors. These were the reasons for my firm belief that our IPO would be a success.

I am basically a technocrat and do not have a profound knowledge of the stock markets. In some cases, ignorance helps. There is a saying, 'Fools will rush into the thick of problems, whereas wise people will shy away from them'. My situation was quite similar to that. Many consultants and analysts asked me, 'Why are you being so reckless and taking your company to the capital markets at a time when even giants have failed. Why should you burn your fingers knowing well that you are playing with fire?'.

Our Chairman Mr. P.G.R. Prasad, Independent and Non-Executive Director Mr. C.J. George, and former Non-Executive Director Mr. R. Krishna Iyer, who knew our company's inner strength, gave me tremendous support, and that boosted my morale. The outcome of our IPO has once again convinced us that the name V-Guard is deeply rooted in the hearts of millions of people. The fact that, despite adverse market conditions, the retail sector was subscribed more than 4 times, with more than 40 thousand applicants, bears ample testimony to that. I usually find an opportunity in every difficult situation. In this instance, the name V-Guard has become more popular and gained higher visibility in North India because, to everyone's surprise, a small company from the South ventured into the capital market, at a time when even corporate giants were being uprooted. As far as V-Guard is concerned, this process has helped to project the brand name in various other parts of India, which is equivalent to spending crores of rupees on advertisements. The well-known statement, 'When the sky is the darkest, the stars shine the brightest' came literally true in this case.

33

Worrying breeds ill health

One of the key attributes of great leaders, is their ability to remain calm during a crisis. Most people get upset and agitated in difficult situations. The greatness of a person is measured by the way he or she reacts when problems arise. If we wish to achieve higher goals, we certainly need to encounter great challenges, which may disturb our peace of mind. There is yet another set of people who simply worry for nothing, without knowing the facts.

This reminds me of the story of a king, who was deeply worried and lost sleep when he learnt that an enemy had intruded into his capital

> Worrying about the future and anticipating disasters is certainly not the right approach to life. We must have the strength of mind to declare, 'Come what may'.

Worrying Breeds Ill Health

and was trying to kill him. People living near the palace noticed that the trees in the vicinity had been pierced by a few arrows in various places. Interestingly, all these arrows were located precisely in the centre of a circle of nails that were embedded around each of them. This circle was about four inches in diameter. Upon hearing the news, the king was upset and sent the army chief to verify the facts. The man was surprised to note that the arrows and nails were aligned in such a meticulous fashion.

As far as the king was concerned, this was clear evidence that the intruder wanted to publicly demonstrate his skills as a sharpshooter, and that he wanted to assassinate him. He began to have sleepless nights, worrying that his life was in real danger. Soldiers were sent to capture the intruders, but during the first few weeks, their efforts were in vain. A few new arrows could be spotted on the trees.

However, one day the soldiers managed to get hold of the culprit. He was just an innocent twelve year old boy, playing with a bow and arrow. The child was tied up and brought to the king's palace. On being questioned about how he accomplished such a feat of marksmanship, the boy revealed the trick. He would first shoot an arrow at a tree, and when it was firmly in position, he would carefully draw a circle, keeping the arrow precisely in the centre. He would then drive a few nails in the tree, exactly on the circumference of this circle. When the king asked the boy why he did this, he replied innocently, 'Just for fun. That is all.'

The king was greatly relieved to hear this. He had worried unnecessarily, thinking that he would encounter a formidable enemy, without knowing the facts. In our day-to-day lives, there are times when we start worrying about matters which have no factual basis. People in all walks of life know full well that life is full of challenges. Worrying about the future, anticipating disasters is certainly not the right approach to life. We must have the strength of mind to declare, 'Come what may'.

34

Persevere and Win

There is a saying, 'If you are not making mistakes, then you are not making decisions'. What this really means is that decision making requires past experience, and in order to acquire experience, you need to try out various options. In that process, there are bound to be failures. A true leader always likes to walk through uncharted territory, which will present many hidden challenges. Starting any new venture is like walking through unknown territories.

Never lose the will to win, even in the midst of failure

Persevere and Win

As a leader, you have to take calculated risks. Great leaders do not worry about their mistakes; they learn lessons from them. If we realize why we failed the last time, we can succeed the next time. However, we should take care not to repeat the same mistake. Leaders have the courage to take action where others hesitate. There must be an urge to win even in utterly hopeless circumstances. Many of you may have heard the story of King Robert Bruce, who was defeated six times in a row, when he went to war with a neighbouring country. He was finally cornered and was hiding in a cave, where he noticed a spider spinning a web. He saw that it was jumping quite a distance from one corner to another, in order to fix the first main string of its web. Although it failed several times, the spider made repeated attempts, instead of giving up.

The king watched the spider with great curiosity. It failed six times but persistent effort helped it succeed the seventh time! The King thought to himself, "I too have failed six times already, but I am bound to win the seventh time". He mobilized his soldiers secretly and history testifies that he won the battle the next time. The moral of the story is, 'Never lose the will to win, even in the midst of failure'.

Subordinates eagerly await directions from their leader, and they will show greater enthusiasm to work under a leader who is willing to take risks. Such leaders will give their subordinates more freedom and allow them to try out various options. Moreover, such leaders will not blame their juniors, even if mistakes are committed in the course of a new venture. The strength of leaders can be assessed by measuring how comfortable they are in addressing difficult situations.

35
Curiosity helps Innovate

Our attitude can change the course of our lives and even turn defeat into victory. We must be emotionally stable in difficult situations. This can be achieved only if we face challenges and pass through failures. A pessimist will find a difficulty in every opportunity, while an optimist will perceive an opportunity in every difficulty.

The invention of 'Velcro', a fabric hook-and-loop fastener, was facilitated by a simple but amazing incident. Its inventor George de Mestral was walking through a field, on his way back home after a hunting trip, when he noticed that the seeds of a particular type of plant were sticking to his pants in large numbers. He literally had to pluck them out one by one, but never got irritated or lost patience. He noticed that all of them were of the same shape and size, and was inquisitive to learn how these seeds could have such a firm grip on his

> We have to be inquisitive, and need to remember that opportunities lie hidden even in a blade of grass.

clothes. He collected a few samples and analyzed them, first with a magnifying glass and later under a microscope. The hooking pattern of those seeds was eventually adopted for the invention of Velcro, which is today a very popular and relatively inexpensive method of binding two materials reversibly, in a simple fashion.

The message conveyed through this incident, is that we have to be inquisitive, and need to remember that opportunities lie hidden, even in a blade of grass! But, to be able to observe patiently, we must first of all remain calm and cool at the inconvenience caused in a given predicament. The discovery of penicilin tells us a similar story. Normally, people in such situations would get annoyed and miss the opportunity of discovering a new idea. It is better to light a candle than to curse the darkness. There are people who always come out with bright ideas, and there are some who always come out with bright excuses!

There is a saying, 'Success is a journey not a destination'. Anyone who is successful will strive for it incessantly. Such people do not rest contented with just one success. Even when they meet failures along the way, they will persist until circumstances turn in their favour to make their ventures successful. The public may say that such people are lucky and have the 'Midas touch' without taking into account the amount of hard work and perseverance that lies behind such achievements.

I have never believed in luck. In my opinion, it plays only a minor role in success. If there is good luck today, there will be ill-luck tomorrow. So how can we depend on it? If you say that George de Mestral, the inventor of Velcro just happened to be lucky, I cannot agree with you. You and I had similar opportunities, but he alone had the acumen to perceive the potential for a big initiative in a small thing. In Malayalam there is a saying 'Kannundayal pora kaananam'. It means 'It is not enough that you have eyesight, you need to use them to observe things properly'.

36

Effective Communication

One important quality which all leaders share in common, is their ability to motivate their subordinates with encouraging words. The ability to convince others effectively is essential, and is found in abundance in all successful personalities. The way we express ourselves is more important than what we say. This is equally applicable to written communication too.

I am reminded of the story of a blind boy, who was begging on the pavement. He had a board displayed in front of him, which read, 'I am blind, Please help me', and had a towel spread out to collect coins. Only a few coins lay on the towel. A gentleman who was watching this closely, decided to change the situation. With the boy's permission he

> The ability to convince others effectively is essential, The way we express ourselves is more important than what we say.

rewrote the words on the board as follows : 'What a beautiful day it is! Unfortunately, I am unable to enjoy it, because I am blind'.

The man then waited a few metres away to watch the response of the public. The new wording moved the heart of many people and many coins fell on the towel! Whoever had read the board thought, 'How lucky I am!, Unlike this boy I am able to see'. A good example of motivating people to do good!

The moral of the story is very simple. Through calculated and purposeful communication, we can convince or motivate people! Communication is an integral part of any organization. When a large number of people are working in an organization and decision-making is done in various parts of the country, the role of proper communication is vital. In many cases, subordinates commit mistakes owing to lack of precision in the instructions given by the superiors. Unless superiors properly convey their expectations and verify how well their instructions have been understood, subordinates are likely to commit mistakes. In such cases, it is most unjust to put the blame on them.

Many seniors are impatient and in a hurry while communicating with their subordinates. It is only natural that the latter will get confused when instructions are conveyed in haste. In Malayalam there is a saying 'Chakka ennu paranjhal Chukk ennu Manasilaakum', which means, 'If you say jackfruit they will understand it as dried ginger'. I usually explain things in great detail to my subordinates, irrespective of whether he is a peon, a driver or a manager. I know that sometimes the listener may get bored, but I don't mind that, since I am mainly concerned with whether they clearly understand what I am saying.

There are polite ways to express your dissent on a particular subject. One should refrain from using harsh words, which can spoil the situation and then the relationship. In short, communication should be precise and unequivocal as it is an area of supreme importance in any walk of life.

37
Presence of Mind

One day, a landlord placed an advertisement in the newspaper, to find a suitable caretaker for his farmhouse. The selected candidate would have to look after the cattle and poultry, the farmhouse and so on. The challenge was that the location was notorious for severe hurricanes and storms. So, no one was willing to come forward to take up that job. The lone candidate who responded to the advertisement, said during the interview, 'Sir, I can sleep well, even in the midst of a storm or a hurricane!'.

Although the landlord was puzzled by such a response, he appointed the man as the caretaker. Late one night, a radio announcement forecast severe hurricane and thunderstorms in that region. The landlord immediately telephoned the caretaker and informed him about the storm warning. However, the man was undisturbed by the news and replied, 'Sir, I had told you during the interview that I can sleep well, even if there is a hurricane and storm.

> One common trait that we find in successful people, is their ability to face challenges with equanimity and maturity.

Presence of Mind

Good night.' The landlord was annoyed with the reply and regretted having selected such a lazy man.

He immediately mobilized a few workers and rushed to the farmhouse, which was a two hour drive from his house. On reaching there, he was surprised to find that everything was well-protected and intact. Although the hurricane was fierce, the caretaker had remained cool and did everything needed without losing his presence of mind during the crisis. He had already covered the grains storage with extra tarpaulin sheets, moved the cattle and poultry to safer places, and everything was intact even after the big storm.

Only now did the landlord realize the implications of what the caretaker had said during the interview. He had intended to convey that he would remain cool and retain his presence of mind during any crisis situation. The purpose of narrating this story is to emphazhise the importance of retaining one's presence of mind in difficult situations. One common trait that we find in successful people, is their ability to face challenges with equanimity and maturity. Some people show extraordinary courage in extremely difficult situations. Others will respect such people, who will eventually be elevated to leadership positions. Many will look to them for guidance. Hero-worship is a natural instinct in man and those who evince courage in crisis are always looked upon with awe and reverence.

Some people are born with amazing self-confidence and courage. It is my firm belief that we can train ourselves to be courageous in difficult situations. If we want to learn swimming, we have to literally get into the pool. We will not be able to swim, by merely attending detailed lectures on swimming. Similarly, if we wish to develop self-confidence and courage, we have to encounter a series of difficult situations, both big and small. I like to read articles on 'how to confront crisis situations', 'how to tide over difficult situations, etc.' so that I can prepare my mind to face similar challenges.

38

Calm in a Storm

The ability to stay calm and composed in crisis situations is essential for success in life. I firmly believe that we can train ourselves to be stable and calm in difficult situations. In Malayalam there is a saying, 'Paalam kulunghiyaalum Kelan kulughilla', which literally means, 'Even if the bridge is shaken, some people will not despair or get worried, which shows their inner strength.'

We often come across people who appear healthy and robust, but who get frightened over little set-backs. Conversely, some people who look frail and weak, demonstrate extraordinary courage in difficult situations. So, physical strength is not a real criterion of inner strength. There are also people who maintain their poise and remain

> If we are in deep trouble, it is better to look at the lighter side of the issue, which helps to ease our worries.

cool in difficult times. We too can develop such an attitude through persistent efforts and build up inner strength by saying to ourselves, 'I will survive as I have the strength and determination to overcome any difficulty'. Franklin Roosevelt once said, 'The only thing we have to fear is fear itself.'

Many people tend to exaggerate the dimensions of even a very small problem. We have to assess each problem on its merits. In many cases, the worst that is feared when it occurs, will not be as bad as we apprehended. We can keep busy on other matters to stop ourselves dwelling on our problems. If I have a serious problem, I divert my attention to a new project. This has a dual advantage. It will reduce the intensity of the existing problem and at the same time, since the mind is extra alert, it can generate unique ideas for the new project.

If we are deep in trouble, it is better to look at the lighter side of the issue, which helps to ease our worries. We come across people with extraordinary mental courage, who can crack jokes even in the midst of a crisis. We can learn and practise how to calm a troubled mind, and banish unwanted thoughts. Beware that in times of difficulties we get easily agitated, and the consequence is that we are likely to blow up the problem out of proportion, which, in turn, adversely affects our capacity to face it. We must learn to accept the inevitable failures occasioned by unforseeable circumstances. Everyone will have to encounter problems. But we have a tendency to entertain the false notions such as 'The grass appears greener on the other side of the fence' or, 'The neighbor's wife is always beautiful.'

Success is a blend of courage, determination and perseverance. Twenty-seven years of imprisonment did not diminish the spirit of Nelson Mandela! He finally succeeded in his mission, and for the first time in history, a black man became the president of South Africa. So, hold on to your courage, determination and perseverance. Success will be yours.

39

Knock at all doors, armed with a warm heart

A ship at sea developed a technical snag in its engine and had to halt in a harbor for repairs. The engineers on board could not repair it and they sought the help of an expert. It was a fact that the ship was very old, and there were very few experts who could do the job. Eventually, the crew and their agents located an old mechanic, whose services

> To overcome difficult times, we have to try various options and sometimes we need to walk through uncharted territory

81

were in great demand for repairing old engines. Although the man was known to charge exorbitantly for his services, he was invited to repair the ship.

The old man went aboard the ship with a few spanners and a hammer. After a detailed study of the engine, he tapped thrice with his hammer, on a particular part of the engine. To everyone's surprise, the engine started up and began working perfectly! The whole process took less than an hour and everyone was happy. When he was asked to submit his bill, the man simply wrote on a white paper, 'Ship engine repair charges - 10,000 dollars'!

The captain of the ship was shocked to see the ten thousand dollar charge for a job that took less than an hour to complete. So he asked for a detailed, item-wise bill. The mechanic re-submitted his bill, on a slightly larger piece of white paper as, 'Cost of tapping thrice with a hammer: 100 dollars, Cost of knowing where to tap : 9,900 dollars', adding up to a total of ten thousand dollars!

The moral of the story is that success in life depends on one's problem-solving ability. Our competence will improve if we are able to tackle intricate issues by spotting their roots. Everyone faces problems in his/her day-to-day life. When we look around, we see that no one is an exception to this. A close observation of successful people will show that the ability to solve various problems which come up in day-to-day life, is a prominent quality in their character. Within an organization, the subordinates will readily accept such people as their leaders.

To excel in life we need to come out of our comfort zone. A one-year-old child learns to walk, only after falling down several times. Similarly, in order to become an expert in problem-solving, we need to encounter many issues, some of which may be beyond our ability to tackle. But this should not discourage us because failures are truly the stepping-stones to success. If we intend to improve ourselves, we need to learn lessons from our failures. When we encounter problems, we must have a cool head and a warm heart. An agitated and frustrated mind will just add fuel to the fire, and the situation at hand will only get worse. A cool head, a balanced mind will help us take a mature decision.

To instill confidence into our colleagues in crisis situations, what we need is a warm heart, and a friendly and supportive attitude towards them. To overcome difficult times, we have to try various options and sometimes we need to walk through uncharted territory. And for this, a cool head and a warm heart are essential. So, develop the ability to maintain a 'Cool head and a warm heart'. Success is certain.

40

Professional Commitment

I was moved to tears when I read a news item relating to the Bombay terror attack. It showed how Mr. Karambir Kang (40), the General Manager of Taj Mahal Palace Hotel, displayed superhuman courage and dedication to his job, when he continued to supervise rescue operations for over 60 hours, despite the loss of his immediate family members in the tragic incident. His wife Nitti (38), sons Samar (14) and Uday (5) perished in the fire that gutted several rooms and floors of the hotel.

> Commitment towards the profession is the main reason for my success in life.

Ordinary human beings cannot do their duties in the midst of such shock and it calls for extra-ordinary commitment, dedication and sincerity to remain calm and composed in such a precarious predicament. The next day when Ratan Tata visited the devastated hotel, he was surprised to see that Karambir was there to receive him. Speaking to CNN, Ratan Tata said that when he had offered his condolences, Kang had replied: 'Sir, you know we are going to beat this. We are going to build this Taj back to what it was. We are standing by you. We will not let this event take us down.'

This demonstrates the height of commitment, dedication and courage to which one can rise. The fact that the Taj Hotel was able to resume operations within two months after the incident is a glowing tribute to the sterling qualities of the hotel's personnel. I take this opportunity to pay homage to the departed souls and salute the dedication and commitment of Mr. Karambir Kang, although I do not know him personally.

This reminds me of an incident that happened in my own life. It was on 28th August, 1978, the day my son Arun was born. It was a Monday, and my wife Sheela was at her brother's house in Trichur when labour pains began. I had been with my parents at Parappur earlier on Sunday night, and was waiting at Trichur railway station on Monday morning at 8.30 a.m., to board the train to Ernakulam, when Sheela's brother arrived there and conveyed to me that she had been admitted to hospital.

When I reached the hospital, Sheela was already in the labour room. Taking stock of the situation, Sheela's mother and two sisters, her sister in-law and two brothers were already there on the veranda, extending their service. The nurses would not allow me to enter the labour room, but I learned from the junior doctors that everything was normal and that it may take four to six hours for the delivery. Since I had no specific role there, my mind was drawn to certain commitments, back at my office in Cochin.

Professional Commitment

During those days V-Guard was practically a one-man show, and I had to manage various functions, including marketing, accounts, production and purchasing, with only a clerk to assist me. The total staff strength was only eleven at that time. On that particular Monday, I had committed to the raw material suppliers that I would be issuing them a few cheques. I also needed to deposit some cheques at the bank lest those cheques mentioned above should go dishonoured. But my cheque book and the cheque leaves to be deposited, were all locked up in my table and the key was with me.

Without explaining the situation in detail to Sheela's brother, I quietly slipped away from the hospital, came to Cochin by a public transport bus, performed my duties and got back to Trichur within five hours. By then, Arun had already been born. Without knowing the facts of the matter, Sheela expressed her displeasure against my conduct. The misunderstanding was cleared up later. I firmly believe that my commitment towards the profession accounts for my success in life.

41
The Conquest of Fear

While interacting with a group of MBA students, I was asked a very pertinent question, 'Sir, during your career, what steps did you take to improve your self-confidence?' I responded to it in some detail, backing up my points with numerous examples. During my college days I was a little reserved and was only an average student. But, as my business progressed, out of sheer necessity I was compelled to address various groups such as our marketing executives and dealers. When I noticed that I was not very effective as a public speaker, I decided to join various training programs, which could improve my skills.

> Our lives will expand in direct proportion to our willingness to improve our skills and overcome weaknesses.

In fact, I attended three or four such programs of various types, which definitely improved my public speaking skills, and I noticed that I was also growing in self-confidence. I began to read books on self-motivation and management thoughts of eminent personalities. Again as the business progressed further, I realized that my knowledge of accountancy and commerce was inadequate, and that I was ill-equipped to understand the intricacies of financial statements such as balance sheet, profit and loss account and so on. In order to overcome that, I attended a six months' part-time coaching class on the subject, conducted by a chartered accountant. I also attended a number of personality development training programs to improve my soft skills. On the whole, all these efforts helped me to improve my self-confidence considerably.

In my opinion, our lives will expand in direct proportion to our willingness to improve our skills and overcome weaknesses. A man was suffering from a fear of heights, a condition known as acrophobia. Do you know how he overcame his fear? He joined the flying club! He overcame his fear by flying the aircraft during the high altitude training programs. I learned swimming at the age of 42. Until then I was afraid of deep waters. All the others taking the swimming lessons with me were young children, and I was the only adult. Even though it took me a long while to master swimming skills, I am now happy that I no longer fear deep waters!

When we study the lives of successful people, we come to know that their ability to surmount problems is the main contributory factor for their success. They show amazing courage during difficult situations. When faced with failure, we must have the courage to say, 'I will try again'. Then the question remains : 'how do you acquire courage?' My answer is: 'look within and discover your hidden potential'. A wise man once said, 'Within me is infinite power, before me is endless possibility, around me is boundless opportunity - why should I fear?'

42

Lessons from the recession

The world which we live in is full of challenges, conflicts, confusion and uncertainties. Good times and hard days come around often, and no one can make accurate predictions about the future. Until October 2008, we boasted that we were lucky to live in the 21st century, at a time when the world economy was growing rapidly, and that India and China would emerge as the economic giants of the new fast changing world. We are now suddenly forced to deal with new threats and still worse, a global recession, which no one was able to predict a decade ago. Many have asked me about my attitude towards the current crisis.

> Hard days come from time to time, and I believe it is like a grinding stone which will polish our skills. It helps us to acquire more knowledge and build up greater self-confidence. Our minds will be more alert and we will see things in their right perspective, which will help us find solutions to various vexing problems.

Lessons from the Recession

My view on these developments is a balanced one, 'Certain things have to happen at certain times'. Let me quote again from the Bhagavathgeetha, 'Sambhavaami yuge yuge', which means 'whatever will be, will be'. What we need to do, is to accept the situation. Acceptance is neither inaction nor sitting quiet, but implies looking for the blessings in disguise in the face of adversity, for every cloud has a silver lining 'Life does not directly give you what you want, but you have to churn out what you need'.

Hard days come from time to time, and I believe it is like a grinding stone, which will polish our skills. It helps us to acquire more knowledge and build us greater self-confidence. Our minds will be more alert and we will see things in their right perspective, which will help us find solutions to various vexing problems. We must maintain a cool head in difficult times. Remember the saying: 'The good makes no noise and noise does no good'.

When I reflect on the impact of the so-called recession, I would say that it has come as a blessing for us, helping us to cut down unwanted expenditure and to find ways to implement cost effective methods in production, distribution and marketing. We could drastically reduce our advertisement expenditure by adopting new strategies without affecting the brand image. We tightened finance and inventory so that profits remained the same as that of last year. Another great advantage of the recession is that many competitors who produced inferior quality products, and followed unethical marketing tactics have been eliminated.

For the reasons cited above, I am, in fact, happy that I could witness a major global recession during my lifetime, which is indeed a rare opportunity. It is my firm belief that 'No matter what situation we have to face, we are responsible for the way we react'. During a crisis we must be more careful with the words we use and the decisions we make. To have clarity in thought, we must be in a calm state of mind. In any situation, it is always better to maintain sobriety and equanimity.

43

Synergy I

An eight year old boy once went to a beach, for the first time in his life. He was accompanied by his parents and they played with the waves for quite a while. The boy was thrilled to see the waves and experience the force with which they hit the beach. When he had finished playing with the waves and was about to leave, the boy noticed an empty mineral water bottle lying on the beach. He picked it up and filled it with sea water. Noticing this, his father asked him, 'What are you going to do with this water?' The boy replied, 'I love sea water very much and I want to take some home.'

As soon as the boy reached home, he emptied the contents of the bottle into a bucket. He then keenly watched the water and seemed to be waiting anxiously to see something happening. After

> The success of a team depends on the way the members share common ideals and embrace a common goal. Regardless of differences, members strive shoulder-to-shoulder, confident in one another's faith, trust and commitment.

some time, the boy approached his father tearfully and said, 'The sea water which I brought here, is not making any waves in the bucket.' Having seen the waves at the beach, the boy had mistakenly believed that sea water would generate waves, wherever it is! With a smile on his face the father explained, 'Dear son, the water gets the energy only when it is in the sea. When we remove it from there, it loses its energy and is unable to produce waves.' The father went on to give the boy a detailed explanation, which pacified him.

Organizations and individuals can be compared with the mighty ocean and its water. Water gets the strength only when it is part of the ocean. As we know, water in the sea is extremely powerful and it can generate a lot of energy. The same principle can be applied to the staff members within an organisation. The moment a little water is taken out from the sea and placed in a bucket, it loses its energy and remains still. Similarly, individuals lose their energy and space, the moment they cease to be part of the organisation. I am a person who has really witnessed the power of teamwork. V-Guard was literally a one-man show in the initial days. Now, after 32 years, it has grown big and I believe that the team spirit manifested in concerted effort is the real driving force behind the success.

The main crux of teamwork revolves round the slogan, 'We believe in each other. and rely on each other' The success of a team depends on the way the members share common ideals and embrace a common goal. Regardless of differences, the members strive shoulder-to-shoulder, confident in one another's faith, trust and commitment. If the team is vibrant and active we can literally experience the above qualities. The duty of a team leader is to create a feeling of belongingness among the members, and to develop team spirit. In the long run it can work wonders. Leaders may keep in mind that, the "Do what I say" approach is against the basic concept of teamwork.

44

Synergy II

Whether it is a business organization, a political party or any group of people with a common objective, it is imperative to create team spirit among the members, without which it cannot attain growth and strength. The primary duty of the leader, is to create an atmosphere, conducive to the personal growth of individuals within the organization.

Nowadays, youngsters have enormous opportunities that may induce them to leave an organization to take up a job elsewhere. So the focus of the top level managers should be, to find ways to create a strong feeling of belongingness among the staff members. Team

> The duty of the leader, is to create an atmosphere conducive to the personal growth of individuals within the organization.

spirit is directly proportionate to the feeling of belongingness within the group. If the sense of belongingness is weak, it is only natural that the team spirit will be low, and vice versa. I believe that top level managers have a vital role to play in creating a congenial atmosphere within the organization.

It is also the prime responsibility of the leader to create a synergic atmosphere among the staff members. He should be fully aware that people under him are responsible for his position. For example, a Managing Director must be ever concious of the fact that the executive chair that he occupies, is being lifted up and held in that high position by his managers and staff members. The more these members are charged and enthused, the more elevated will the Managing Director's chair be.

Building a strong and vibrant organization simply means building an efficient and homogeneous team of people. If the HOD's are performing well, then the respective departments will be delivering good results. The ability to influence and convince people is a crucial factor in building efficient organizations. When we deal with people, just remember that they are as delicate, as you are ! The first principle we have to follow is, 'Be true to yourself and considerate of others'.

If we wish to teach the importance of hard work or straightforwardness to our subordinates, we must first be true to ourselves, and put these ideals into practice in our own lives. Our children and subordinates are continuously and closely watching our deeds rather than just listening to our words. So if we want to teach them a particular mode of action, we must first be a living example to them. Mahatma Gandhi said, 'My life is my message.' Since he lived an ideal life , many people emulated him and became dedicated followers. It goes without saying that preaching unbacked by practice is an exercise in futility.

45

Effective Delegation

The success of team building is directly proportionate to the top management's willingness to delegate. The art of delegation is the most important skill of a manager or a leader. But many find it difficult or even inconvenient, to get others to do things. Sometimes, even efficient people are apprehensive or skeptical about delegation of powers. They

> The advantage of effective delegation is that it will reduce our work pressure and stress, while ensuring that the task is completed in time. It will enable the leader to utilise most of his time, skill and energy for planning and strategy development.

Effective Delegation

underestimate the ability of their subordinates. Yet another set of managers believe that the quickest way of getting something done, is to do it themselves. Some are perfectionists, and they spend a great deal of time getting involved in trivial issues and actually end up in doing the job themselves.

Some managers are wary of delegating tasks and are reluctant to share information with their subordinates, fearing that their position in the organization will be undermined, if they do so. A conscientious manager must realize that, for the overall growth of the organization, delegation is essential. In order to successfully delegate a task, we must make sure that the person to whom the task is being delegated, is not only competent but well informed about what is expected of him/her. We should also give them the authority and the resources they need, to get things done.

The leader must keep an eye on the over-all progress of work, and give proper guidance from time to time. He must also be willing to accept responsibility for the outcome of the task. Delegation will be effective, only with a lot of preparation and planning. During this phase, a leader must give his subordinates a lot of support and guidance so as to instil confidence in them to take up the task. But when the time comes for actually executing the given task, he should allow them the maximum freedom. It is necessary to give them an idea about timelines and deadlines, well in advance. Any last minute rush will affect the quality of the work.

It is always better to explain the task at hand to all the team members, so that everyone is well-informed about the diverse aspects of the mission. Once your team has been given a thorough picture of the task, you should refrain from interfering in their work and looking into minute details. Unnecessery and incessant intervention conveys a wrong message, that you have no faith in their capabilities. Continuous involvement and intervention at each step violates the basic principles of delegation. Focus on results and grant them maximum flexibility in the process of execution.

A perfectionist is likely to fail in the art of delegation. If you have no faith in your subordinates, then delegation will not yield good fruits, positive results. Team building entails giving your subordinates greater responsibility, thereby empowering them to accomplish difficult tasks. The advantage of effective delegation is that it will reduce work pressure and stress, while ensuring that the task is completed in time. It will enable the leader to utilize most of his time, skill and energy for planning and strategy development.

46
Coping with grief

It is heartbreaking for bereaved family members to reconcile themselves to the untimely and sudden demise of their beloved ones. However, we have to accept the fact that death is the only certain reality in this uncertain world, and yet, when it strikes us we get depressed and dejected. We need to develop courage and mentally condition ourselves to tide over such inevitable situations.

This reminds me of an incident in the life of Gautam Buddha. One day a lady approached him, crying aloud and pleaded, "Oh my Lord, I have just lost my only son. He was the only hope in my life.

> If we can mentally prepare ourselves in advance, we can minimize the trauma and shock caused by such eventualities.

My Lord, I have great faith in you and I am sure that you can bring my son back to life.

I know that you can work miracles. I have great faith in you and I am sure that you can bring him back to life. Without him, my life has no meaning and I no longer have the desire to continue living". The Buddha's efforts to console her were in vain because she was totally unwilling to accept the reality. He then said to her, "Yes, I can resurrect your son, but on one condition; you have to find and bring me one spoonful of mustard from a house where no death has occurred. None of the members of that household should have lost any of their loved ones earlier. If you can do this, your son can be saved".

With great hope the lady ran from house to house, to find one which met these conditions and to collect a spoonful of mustard from there. She went all around the village but her efforts were not fruitful. She could not find a single house where no death had occurred. By then she had begun to realize that death is an inevitable phenomenon. She came across several people whose condition was much worse than hers. Finally, she reconciled herself to the loss of her son and lived peacefully thereafter.

Accidents, terminal diseases, major setbacks and death are all an inevitable part of life, and could happen to you and me. We have to learn to come to terms with reality, when such things happen in our lives. There is a practice among Christians to write a message on coffins, "Today it is me, tomorrow it may be your turn". What a pertinent note of caution! All of us agree that death is inevitable, but we believe that it will not happen to us in the near future. Although painful, there is a way to acquire peace of mind in traumatic situations. Once in a while, visualize that someone dear to us is a victim of such incidents. If we can mentally prepare ourselves in advance, we can minimize the trauma and shock caused by such eventualities.

47

A need for Civic Sense

Bologna is a place which is about an hour's flight away from the famous city of Milan, the commercial capital of Italy. We visited the largest amusement park of Italy, called 'GardaLand', which is only an hour's drive from where we were staying.

Garda Land is more than ten times the size of Veega Land and the investment must be several times higher as well. On that particular day a rough estimate I made, indicated that there were around 20,000 visitors in the park. As park operators in India, we were curious about the behaviour of the visitors and the staff there. Even though there were long queues at each attraction, the visitors appeared self-disciplined and no one attempted to violate the rules. In fact, we hardly found any security guards inside the park. Even

Do not cause inconvenience to your co-passengers.

in such a crowded place, there was no litter anywhere in the park. I noticed the father of a 3 year old child quickly picking up a chocolate wrapper that the child had carelessly dropped on the ground, and advising him not to repeat it.

From the time we arrived at the Park, I watched a beautiful lady in expensive clothes, moving around the park with a pet dog. In Europe & the U.S.A. pet dogs are common sights in public places, and form an integral part of life. I was anxious that this dog might spoil the cleanliness of the park. Pretty soon, exactly as I apprehended, right before our eyes, the dog started defecating on the paved tiles. I became a little annoyed and wondered whether western culture only preached about cleanliness without practising it. I watched in disbelief as the lady cleaned up the mess on the pavement using a polythene bag and a bunch of tissues. She then took out a few tissue papers from her bag and meticulously cleaned the pavement. The lady had no reservations whatsoever about doing all this, in front of others. I thought to myself that her sincerity and commitment to society deserved to be appreciated. This act of hers, clearly illustrated the principle, 'Do not cause inconvenience to your co-passengers'.

In sharp contrast, let me narrate an incident that happened in Veega Land recently, which I witnessed. During my daily routine inspection in the park one day I was shocked to see a two year old child relieving himself on the beautiful pathway of the park. His parents seemed to be educated and wealthy. Yet, they simply walked away from the scene, leading the child to the toilet, leaving the excrement on the pathway. This showed how irresponsible and careless they were about the incident. I was very disturbed and had to call our housekeeping staff to clean the area.

Sad to say, this is not an isolated instance of this kind. Even though we Indians claim to have a rich tradition and cultural heritage, I still feel that we are far behind in civic sense, manners and etiquette.

48

Declining Spiritual Values

During a conversation I had with a person who claimed to be a staunch atheist and rationalist, he asked me, "You have stated in your book 'Practical Wisdom Part I', that you have never believed in luck as a major factor in one's success. Yet, the vast majority of businessmen I know, certainly bank on luck, and worship God to receive personal favours." With a little emotion he added, "In general, businessmen have blind faith; they make offerings worth lakhs of rupees to temples, churches and mosques, with a selfish motive to gain more. And yet, they are reluctant to donate to charity and are generally not

> Over a period of many centuries, the old religions became more or less institutionalized, and some of them have lost their sanctity to a great extent.

concerned about the less fortunate. They approach leading astrologers and palmists, spend large amounts of money, seeking more personal fortune and benefits, while simply ignoring the needs of the poor".

His frustration evident, he gave vent to his ire, "Many businessmen donate huge amounts of money to various places of worship to enter into the good books of religious leaders, while evading taxes due to the government. Most often these people are the real decision makers of churches, temples and mosques. He then questioned various religions, accusing them collectively of misguiding people, encouraging superstition and selfishness among people. "Religious leaders are the main culprits, who spoil communal harmony that exists among ordinary, innocent people", he asserted.

At this point I intervened and said that his observations were partially true, but he was taking only a one-sided view of this issue. "I believe that there are many good things in every religion", I said. When we analyze the teachings of the founders of all religions, we find that they carry many valuable messages which can guide people to lead a good life, where one lives in peace and harmony with others, being helpful to them, and causing minimal inconvenience to others. Take the Bhagavad Gita, the Quran, the Holy Bible or any other religious scripture; you will find that all of them carry strong exhortations to promote mutual help, love, peace and happiness. But with the passage of time, and many generations later, these teachings came to be distorted and misinterpreted so much so that the core values which the founders envisaged went unnoticed. Religious leaders today interpret them to their own advantage, whims and fancies. That was why Mahatma Gandhi once said, 'I respect Christ and read the Bible, but I hate Christianity'. He realized that what the majority of Christians practise, is nowhere near the original teachings of Christ. The same applies to all other religions as well.

This is the reason why more people are being drawn to new generation philosophers or prophets, like Sri. Sathya Sai Baba, Sri Sri Ravi Shankar, Matha Amrithanandamayi and so on. Those who live in the present century can relate to these spiritual leaders because they can hear and see what these founders are preaching and doing. Over a period of time, the old or traditional religions became more or less institutionalized and some of them have lost their sanctity to a great extent. But in the case of the new generation religions, the teachings of these spiritual leaders are fresh, genuine, free of distortions, and have a great deal of relevance to present day problems. That is why a large number of people are easily drawn to them. I believe that five or ten, or perhaps twenty centuries after, what happened to the old religions will probably happen to these as well. Finally I concluded the discussion with the thought that if a person gets peace of mind from his or her religion, being inspired to lead a life which is charitable, sensitive and caring for people of all faith, that creed has a genuine claim for acceptance.

49

Faith & Hope Part I

During a heated discussion, on relegion and faith, with a so-called rationalist, he argued that people should think along scientific lines and refrain from following superstitious practices. I replied that those of us who have a good educational background can understand a scientific approach but the majority of people who are illiterate, are more likely to have blind faith in supernatural powers. In my opinion, if people derive peace of mind and happiness by having faith in a higher power,

> If people derive peace of mind and happiness by having faith in a higher power, we should neither interfere in their belief nor try to turn them away from their faith, provided they do not inconvenience others.

we should neither interfere in their belief nor try to turn them away from their faith, provided they do not force their views on others. To illustrate this point, I cited an incident in my life.

While I was studying at college, there lived a poor widow and her only son in our native place, Parappur near Trissur. Her twenty-five year old son was the only breadwinner of the family, who earned a living by doing hard manual labour on daily wages. The illiterate widow was completely dependant on her son, a bachelor then. One day the villagers learnt the shocking news that the young man had been admitted to hospital, where he was diagnosed with the dreadful disease, Leukemia. The villagers began helping her with small amounts of money to meet their food and medical expenses. He was totally bedridden, sometimes at home and sometimes at the hospital. All the villagers were deeply saddened at the fate of the poor widow. But surprisingly, she remained very cheerful and was confident that her son would recover from the disease. Although she did not know what the disease was, she knew that it was a serious one. The temple town of Guruvayoor was only 12 kms away from our place. On the first day of every month of the Malayalam almanac, she would visit the Guruvayoor temple and place a one rupee coin in the 'Hundi', beseeching Sree Krishna to cure her son. After her prayers, she felt reassured and confident that he would recover. This continued for more than a year.

As an educated and curious youngster, who always observed things in a scientific and analytical manner, I closely watched these developments. The question was whether the young man would be fully cured of his disease and could resume a normal life. One day, I discussed this matter with a retired schoolmaster in our village. In the course of our discussion, he clarified. "The issue here is not whether the patient will recover or not. 'Hope' is the driving force of life. If the woman derives strength, courage, hope and peace of mind by going to Guruvayoor and placing a one rupee coin in the 'Hundi', it is well and good. We should not disturb her faith and hope, by arguing and explaining things another way'. He then asked sarcastically, "In this situation, can you suggest an alternative method in science, which will give this widow peace of mind and happiness at the cost of just one rupee?". I was struck by his remark which left a lasting impression on my mind, and the answer was an unhesitating, 'No'.

It was indeed an eye opener for me, because until that moment, I was nursing the impression that only science could provide answers to everything in the universe and that this widow was acting foolishly out of ignorance.

50

Faith & Hope Part II

Months went by, and I closely followed the events in the life of the young cancer patient. In spite of all the prayers of his mother, he finally succumbed to the illness in due course. Yet, to my surprise, the widow continued her trips to Guruvayur temple, saying that all this was God's wish, and that she had no complaints over this. Within a few months of her son's death, she resumed her normal life and went about with a cheerful face. She never complained about or bemoaned her fate, but remained steadfast in her faith in God. I learned a lesson from her, that it is best to take things in our stride and console ourselves during a crisis, or in distressing situations, rather than cursing an adverse fate.

Although most people follow some religion, they have but fragile faith or belief in God. Here is the story of such a man. Once a man fell from a high mountain onto a steep cliff. He somehow managed to hold

> You must have firm conviction in what you believe; otherwise you are heading for trouble.

on to the branch of a tree, which protruded from the cliff. Although he had a strong grip, the branch was very weak and could break at any moment, which could cause him to fall into a deep valley. "O God, save me, save me!" he cried out loudly, asking for God's help. Since the call was so strong and loud, God himself appeared at the bottom of the cliff, hundreds of feet below. Stretching out his arms, God said: 'My dear son, you can jump into my arms. Don't worry, you will be safe in my hands. Jump quickly, I have no time; I'm getting distress calls from different parts of the world, so hurry up'. But the man was reluctant to accept the offer as he wondered whether he would really be in safe hands. God thought: This man has not shown complete faith in me. Why should I waste my valuable time with him, when many others are waiting for my help', and left the place. Whether you are an atheist or a believer in God, you must have firm conviction in what you believe; otherwise you are heading for trouble.

The so-called Rationalist at the end of our discussion, said that these were all debatable points and invited me to the All India Conference of 'Yukthivadi Sangam', which was going to be held at Kollam in Kerala. I was a little hesitant to accept the offer and told him that I had some difference of opinion with the rationalists and wondered whether I would be a misfit in the assemblage. He discussed my concern with the office bearers of the organization, who welcomed my presence and wanted to have a debate on these issues. So I readily agreed.

When the news spread that I was going to address the national conference of rationalists, and when posters carrying my picture appeared on the walls of Kollam town, it raised many eyebrows, and some people even discouraged me from attending the function. Some religious leaders expressed their dislike of my presence at such forums. In my opinion, most rationalists and atheists are people with values and ethics in their personal lives, and are sometimes even more human than those who claim to be religious. They do many good things for society, especially in the campaign for the eradication of superstitions and misconceptions.

51
Faith & Hope Part III

As I entered the hall where the national conference of the 'Yukthivadi sangam' was under way, I was surprised to see that there weren't many participants, perhaps less than two hundred. Since it was an All India Conference, I had expected a very large gathering of delegates at the venue. I said to the organizers, 'If this were a religious retreat or a program organized by a religion, I'm quite sure that there would be thousands of devotees present; perhaps you need to rethink your stance against religion'. During the welcome address it was pointed out that that was the first time a businessman was being invited to speak at their conference. This was because they rarely came across people in the business community who remained uninfluenced by superstitions and religions.

> The need of the hour is to learn to respect other religions

In my talk, I expressed my disagreement with their attitude towards religion. I said that they had no right to blindly oppose all religions and their practices. Narrating the story of the widow in Parappur, I asserted that if people obtained peace of mind, and caused no inconvenience to others in practising their faith, we had to appreciate their efforts and that if they propagated the idea that neither God nor 'the afterlife' exists, then it could have very dangerous consequences. "I know many selfish, arrogant and ruthless people who exploit others even though they call themselves religious. It is only their fear of God and 'life after death' that restrains them from causing more harm to society. If you infuse the non-believer ideology into them, they can cause serious damage to humanity".

"Antagonism towards religion seemed to be the theme of this meet. I surely feel that the messages of the founders of all religions were given only with good intentions; they were quite relevant to the era in which they lived. In course of time, these messages came to be misinterpreted and eventually lost their relevance, or even proved pernicious to both society and nature. Recently, the National Geographic channel showed a program, which demonstrated how the practice of religious monopoly in some parts of Asia, is leading to the extinction of a large number of species of small birds. Centuries ago, the founder of a certain religion preached that even a small act of service to one's fellowmen is more valuable than merely praying to God. He once said, "Instead of praying to God thrice a day, you had better do a little service. For instance, you can help to set free a small bird that is caught in a cluster of thorns; that would count for more, before God". He was a visionary, who taught that we have to serve not just mankind but other species as well".

"As a result, now a large number of small birds are kept caged before the shrines of this religion, and sold at a high price. Devotees buy as many birds as they can afford and set them free, believing that their sins will be pardoned by this gesture. These small birds can survive only if they are in a group, which again must be in a forest. When they are set free, they get scattered and lose their way back to the forest. A detailed study has revealed that these birds die of starvation within three or four days. It is reported that a large underworld gang is at work behind this racket, which includes the capture, confinement and distribution of these birds in different centers. Can you see how the practices of this religion have drifted away from the original message of its founder!"

    I tried my best to convince the rationalists that there are good messages in every religion. Mother Teresa, Fr. Damian and many others were driven by their strong beliefs, which motivated them to serve humanity and get engaged in charitable work. I said that the need of the hour is to learn to respect all religions.

52

Little drops of water create an ocean

Every individual has a commitment to the society in which he or she lives. We can make up a number of lame excuses to evade taxes. But the growth of our country depends on all citizens paying their taxes properly. Some would say, "Even if we pay our taxes promptly and properly, the money will be squandered by a few corrupt politicians and bureaucrats, so why bother to pay tax?". Another group believes that since tax evasion is a regular practice among the majority of people in our country, and is not perceived to be a serious offence, one need not be an honest taxpayer. Yet another group believes that since the government raises huge amounts of money through various taxes, the economy will not be affected if an individual evades tax. But if all individuals begin to think along similar lines, it will adversely

> The progress of a nation is fully dependent on the mindset of its citizens, far more than on its natural resources.

affect the nation, for a country needs a substantial sum of money just for adminstrative purposes and large amounts for development and welfare activitites.

This reminds me of an incident that took place in a village, where a few social workers initiated a milk collection drive, for poor children. They called a meeting of all those families who owned cows, and it was unanimously agreed that each family would donate a glass of milk everyday. It was agreed that before sunrise they would deposit the milk in a big jar that would be kept at the centre of the village. One of the villagers thought, "Since the whole village is contributing, no one is going to find out if I pour water instead of milk, and there is no real harm done. Anyway, they will be able to collect enough milk from the others, and I will have more for my family."

In the gloom of the early morn, they all poured their contributions into the big pot. At the appointed time, when the pot was opened in the presence of all villagers, it was full to the brim, but only with water! Remember that it had been unanimously agreed at the meeting, that each family which owned a cow would donate a glass of milk. But in the end, individual selfishness prevailed, and we saw the result. This incident clearly shows what can happen if everybody starts evading tax.

I firmly believe that the progress of a nation is entirely dependent on the mindset of its citizens, rather than on its natural resources. If everybody decides to evade tax, how can our government find money to invest in poverty alleviation programs, healthcare, education, infrastructure and other development activities? We know that the Government spends huge amounts to maintain a very large force in the tax department to prevent tax evasion, but, in effect, it has become notorious for corruption.

53

Freedom with Responsibility

The seeds of corruption germinate in the hearts of selfish people. If those seeds are allowed to flourish, they will retard the progress of the nation. In a corrupt system, incompetent and selfish people are known to occupy high office and hold powerful positions, and public money gets diverted for personal gains. As a result, the rights of the citizens are violated, and deserving people are denied the help they deserve. When the fence itself eats up the crop, it breeds contempt for the law in society, which, in turn, facilitates the growth of underworld mafia and anti-social elements. This is exactly what is happening in some states in North India.

During one of our visits to the U.S.A., my wife and I spent a good amount of time with a few of our class-mates, who have settled there for fifteen to twenty years. They had completed their college education in India, and worked here for a few years before migrating

> We are yet to learn that freedom should not be allowed to vitiate into licence.

to the US. So they knew the differences between India and the U.S.A. in terms of the quality of democracy and governance. According to them, the laws in that country are very strict, and the human rights are well protected. Democracy does not mean that anyone is free to do anything at any time. For example, if you play loud music at full volume on your audio systems at home between 9 pm and 7am, and if your neighbour lodges a complaint, the police will respond within minutes and have you arrested on criminal charges. Causing inconvenience to others is considered a crime there. I was surprised to hear of it because in our country people have to endure the sound pollution, created by our political parties, temples, churches and mosques, which is truly unbearable. We are yet to learn that freedom should not be allowed to vitiate into licence.

In the US, it is the legal obligation of everyone who lives in a housing complex, to maintain half the width of the road that lies directly in front of his house. Although it is a public road, the portion that passes by one's house should be kept neat and tidy, otherwise the house owner could be in trouble. For example, if a pedestrian drops a plantain peel on your portion of the sidewalk, and later another pedestrian stamps on it and gets injured from a fall, that person can sue you. Over there, they believe that so long as you live in a society, you have certain responsibilities and obligations that go beyond your own immediate circle.

In India, we enjoy excessive freedom. As a result, we are not afraid to violate the law, which itself indicates that the law enforcement mechanisms are inefficient and inadequate. One can get almost anything done here by offering bribes, which has become a common practice. As far as the judicial system is concerned, you have to wait for years to get justice from the courts. Justice delayed is justice denied. Within a democratic setup, everyone has his/her own role to play in making the nation either heaven or hell.

54

The Secret of Good Health

No other axiom is so oft-quoted and widely spread as 'health is wealth'. But most people ignore its wisdom until they fall sick. It is only when the blow strikes that they understand the value and importance of being healthy.

In many cases, we abuse our body in various ways, knowingly or unknowingly. We need to remember that our body is very fragile, and that it needs the following vital nourishments in the required measure, namely food, exercise and rest. Deficiency of any one of these three ingredients, makes our body unfit for carrying out our work, and this is termed as an illness. The human body can get proper rest only if the mind is calm. Unlike animals, the human species is endowed with a unique intelligence, and as a result, all of us tend to worry about the future, in varying degrees. Excessive anxiety about the future is enough to spoil one's health.

> It is a known fact that humans are vulnerable to more illnesses than animals, as they are susceptible to stress and mental tension.

"Since you have no worry about the future I can cure you easily"

Research has revealed that worry, tension and anxiety produce adrenaline in the body and an excess quantity of it, is harmful. In such situations, our muscles, blood vessels and nerves get tightened. The production of adrenaline is our body's natural mechanism to equip us to face dangerous situations. The body cannot get rest when the mind is vexed or agitated. If the mind is agitated, even the costliest bed on earth cannot bring you good sleep. Thus worry, tension and anxiety play a vital role in making a person unhealthy. You might have noticed that those who are mentally strong and are able to keep a cool head, have better health when compared to others, and the converse is equally true.

The maharishis and physicians of ancient India knew the importance of having peace of mind for maintaining good health, which is why, yoga, meditation and relaxation techniques were developed. In one sense, veterenary doctors are fortunate that they only have to treat patients who have no worry, anxiety and tension! So, naturally the treatment will be more effective and recovery will be faster. It is a known fact that humans are vulnerable to more illnesses than animals, as they are susceptible to stress and mental tension. I am emphasizing these aspects, because my personal experience of fifty-seven years has convinced me that tension, worry and anxiety play a major role in causing ill-health.

55
My Role Models I

On 17th April 2004, my father died at the age of 88. He had a peaceful death and I believe that as an individual, he was a very successful man. All his six children are well settled in life, and most of them hold important positions in society. The fact that he was held in very high regard, and was well accepted in the society where he lived, is a clear testimony of his success in life. The local villagers had great respect for him because of his tact, diplomacy and positive outlook on life. I have many childhood memories of people approaching him for advice in solving their day-to-day problems. He was a good listener and extended a helping hand to many people. The presence of a large number of local villagers at his funeral, vouches for their love and affection towards him.

To my mind, the main principles that governed his life were self-discipline and punctuality. He was very systematic in life and

'If you are punctual, time conscious and get into the habit of planning things in advance, you will be successful in life'

My Role Models I

planned everything well in advance. His advice to his children and grandchildren was, 'If you are punctual, time conscious and get into the habit of planning things in advance, you will be successful in life'. He would always remind us that these are the basic qualities needed for a successful person in any walk of life. I have tried my best to emulate his example and firmly believe that this is the main reason for my success. He was very health conscious, which is why he was able to lead a very normal life, except for the last two years.

He led a simple life and was content with limited conveniences and comforts, although he could afford a much higher lifestyle. He used to advise us: 'There is no limit for comfort. If we attain a particular level of comfort, after a while we will yearn for more; this is just a human weakness. To have lasting peace of mind and happiness, control your craving for greater comforts'. This is indeed a valuable piece of advice, even more relevant to life in the modern world. In 1933, when he was 17, he purchased a 'Gillette' shaving razor, made in England. He used it for 70 years. He was so careful in handling it that it still retains its shine, and remains intact. After his death, I brought it home where it is kept in a prominent place, as a valuable souvenir.

When I decided to start a small scale industry to manufacture stabilizers, at the age of 27, most people thought that it was a foolish and immature idea, typical of an impulsive youngster. The banks that I approached, rejected my loan applications outright, stating that a tiny industry could not compete or survive in the market where giants like 'Nelco' and 'Keltron' reigned supreme. However, my father had great confidence in me. He identified my potential and was ready to give me a loan of one lakh rupees. For me, the one lakh rupees which he loaned me, was worth crores. If he had not taken that stand at that point in time, I am sure that the V-Guard group would not have been in existence now!

56

My Role Models II

On 14th November 2006, my mother died at the age of 84. She passed away abruptly without disturbing others much. This was just as she wished, because she firmly believed that one should 'Cause least inconvenience to one's fellow passengers'. One of her good qualities was that she could live with the minimum of conveniences and comforts. It was her opinion that, 'as long as there are crores of starving and needy people in our country, we have no right to lead a luxurious life.' She used to advise us that if we have an excess of money, we should give it away to the poor, rather than spending it on ourselves for pleasure.

Fasting was her hobby, and she made no demands for special foods of any kind. She taught us to adjust with minimum resources, which, in one way, has helped me to adopt cost control habits in my personal life, and in the V-Guard group.

> The richest person in life, is the one who can live a contented life with minimum amenities

Another of her salient qualities was her emotional stability. It was her policy never 'to complain, criticize or condemn', and she was very accommodative and could adapt herself to any situation. She had a high degree of tolerance, and was a courageous and self-confident person, who faced difficult situations with her 'come what may' attitude. I have tried very hard to emulate her qualities, and I believe that I have been partially successful in this regard. If you enquired about her health, she would say, 'I am OK, for a person of my age'. Unlike many other elderly people, she never exaggerated on the condition of her illness. No wonder, even many of our closest relatives did not know that she had been a heart patient for so many years.

In contrast to most other women in our village, she was not talkative, and never indulged in or encouraged gossip. To adopt a well-known adage, she knew fully well that 'the tongue is sharper than the sword!. A two-inch tongue can 'kill' a six feet tall man! In this context, the word 'kill' implies character assassination. So she used it very judiciously. She was well-accepted; many came to her for solace. During my childhood, I often observed that the mother-in-law and the daughter-in-law from the same house, would approach her to ventilate their grievances, because they knew that she would keep their secrets confidential and was quite impartial and cool-headed.

She taught us the importance of hard work and set an example by her own life. In my opinion, she was a workaholic, because she could not sit idle even for a minute. But at the same time, despite her old age, she was able to sit inside a closed room for long hours, in prayer, meditation and reading the Bible. She lived a fully contented life, and I am happy that she had a glorious departure.

57

The Whole Picture

As human beings we have a tendency to complain, criticize and condemn. In general, we always try to see the negative side of things. Right from childhood, we are taught to think in a skeptical manner. Many parents advise their children neither to trust anyone, nor to rely on others. Over a period of years, those children who are brought up this way, will tend to develop a negative orientation in their outlook on life.

All of us like to exaggerate the failings of others, instead of looking at the positive side of things. Many people are fond of idle gossip. Finding fault with others is quite easy, and has become a popular pastime. But to be a leader in society, one must have an optimistic approach, and must be able to see the good and the bad as they are.

> We have to shed all our prejudices against others; only then can we see the real merits in them

The Whole Picture

This reminds me of the story of a Buddhist monk, who was very old and nearing retirement. He decided to appoint his successor and selected six of his best disciples, in terms of their knowledge, communication skills and emotional stability. Having done that, his great task was to find out the most suited one from among them. He called all the six selected disciples together. Drawing a black dot on a white board, he asked them to tell him what they saw. Five of them saw only the black spot. One disciple alone said, 'Sir, what I see is a large space of white, in which there is a small black spot'. He was chosen the successor.

The disciple chosen had the insight to see the whole picture, as it was. The others saw just the negative side, being influenced by a preconceived notion. We have to shed all our prejudices against others; only then can we see the real merits in them. One of the major qualities of real leaders is their positive outlook and the ability to classify the merits and demerits of a given set of circumstances, in the correct proportion.

When I was young, I was in the habit of indulging in negative thoughts and critical of others as any other young person. Later on, I realized that it was necessary to shed such attitudes in order to be successful in life. With this objective in mind, I took pains to attend many personality development programs, which helped me to develop a more positive outlook. Today, I am happy to say that I am a totally changed person. Whatever success, that I may have achieved in my life is mainly the result of my positive attitude and the ability to see things in their correct perspective, without any bias.

58

Happiness Lies Within I

One of our associates, who has known me quite well for over twenty years, recently remarked, 'You always look cheerful and happy. I notice that even during a crisis, you are able to remain cool and can crack jokes. What is the secret of maintaining such a serene outlook?'. I firmly believe that having a happy and smiling face can solve fifty percent of one's problems. We can actually train ourselves to be happy even in difficult situations.

All along my career, I have developed a habit of observing pleasant and cheerful people. Many of them have to deal with serious difficulties in their lives. Some of them are physically handicapped,

> The happiness in our lives, depends on the totality and the quality of our thoughts.

some are facing financial difficulties, and some others are burdened with family problems. They still manage to be happy. From this it is clear that external factors are not the cause of unhappiness. Happiness develops within ourselves. Some people say, 'I would like to be happy, but I can't!'. We must accept situations and must try to be happy even under the worst conditions. Happiness breeds happiness; it is contagious. But you and I will have to make a conscious effort to make this possible.

Worry often casts a big shadow over a small thing. Unhappy people always tend to dislike their present condition. They keep saying, 'Olden days were good; childhood days were better; college days were fun' and so on. But we must be happy with the circumstances and facilities that we have now. Learn to accept sorrows and failures, which is the sole and surest means of attaining happiness.

From time immemorial, mankind has been searching for shortcuts to attain happiness. All religions hold out various ways for us to reach that level. Yet the vast majority of people are unhappy. One night, two people were looking outside through the same window. One of them complained about the darkness and was unhappy. The other looked up and was struck with the beauty of the glittering stars. It is only natural that this person will remain happy throughout his life both in weal and woe. If you can change yourself, or rather your attitude, your life will change on its own.

The happiness in our lives, depends on the totality and the quality of our thoughts. Life is a series of events, full of discord and disharmony. The way in which we respond to these heterogenous situations determines our happiness. Many problems will either subside on their own, or their intensity will become less within a few days or weeks. If we realize and accept this propensity to gain equanimity, we will nurture hope for 'tomorrow'. It is only a confident and optimistic outlook of the mind that makes a man happy.

59

Happiness Lies Within II

I have often disclosed that I value peace of mind more than wealth. As an entrepreneur, there have been numerous occasions which have snatched away my peace of mind. But somehow I have succeeded in regaining calm in those difficult situations, within the shortest possible time. It is indeed an art worth learning at any cost.

A journalist once asked me, ' Did you follow the principles of 'Vasthu' when you constructed your house?' I replied that I have never believed in 'Vasthu', and that all places on earth are good for living. The occupants of a house can make it hell or heaven. It is quite possible for a person living in a hut to be happier than his neighbor who lives in a bungalow. Happiness is within the reach of everyone if only one makes an honest effort to get at it. True happiness comes

> Happiness is attained not by acquiring objects, but by ideas, thoughts and attitudes

from our inner self, and it would be a grave mistake to look for it in the external world. The essence of mental peace is to be able to calm your heart, in the midst of all the turmoil of daily life. In the modern world of competition and speed, everyone is seeking an answer to the question, 'How can we live here in a way that will bring us satisfaction, peace and a sense of meaning?'. If we gain the right insight into what distinguishes happy people from others, we are most likely to attain the goal.

It is matter of common experience that when people are happy, it is reflected on their faces, and they age at a slower rate. Happy people can think better, perform better, feel better and look better. Happy people like themselves and as a natural corollary, they like the society. In turn, they are liked by the society. A pleasing personality radiates charm and wins popularity. Happy people are esteemed in society, and we are naturally drawn towards such people. Happiness is attained not by acquiring objects, but by ideas, thoughts and attitudes. If we believe that our happiness is conditional on others changing their attitudes, then we will never attain it. Please remember that no one can change another person unless he/she feels the need to change . We get satisfaction by creating something, giving something and doing something. Doing something you like, other than a routine office job, will boost your energy. Filling your mind with thoughts of peace, courage and hope will keep you pleasant, even in difficult situations. For the sake of your peace of mind, avoid thinking about people you do not like. The mind is efficient only when it thinks positive. So cultivate a habit of developing inner peace. Unpleasant thoughts on a continuous basis can make us sick. Happiness is not a destination you reach, but a journey. The fundamental truth is that we cannot make others happy if we ourselves are unhappy.

60

Honesty Pays

A king had five senior courtiers, all of whom were intelligent and capable. He decided to select and promote one of them as a minister. The king expressed his wish and gave them a test. He told them, 'I have a few selected seeds of various flowering plants. You can take one each, and also take a pot in which you can grow them into healthy flowering plants at home. After four months, bring your flowerpots to the palace. The one who has the best flowering plant will be selected as the minister. Do not disclose the progress of your plants to each other.'

Each person took home a seed and a pot and began nursing the plant. One of them was shocked to see that despite good care and attention, the seed in his pot never germinated. He was very sincere, hardworking and intelligent, but was saddened by the fact that he did not have a plant. They had been instructed not to discuss the progress of their plants among themselves.

> Honesty is very important when we climb the ladder of success

129

After four months, it was time for the King to make his choice. Four of them had brought their flowering pots to the palace, but one person had only an empty pot to show. When the King came for the inspection, the four who had good plants were eloquent in highlighting their achievement and commenting on the fragrance of the flowers. The man who came with his empty pot was sad, and stood some distance away, reluctant to show himself. When the king reached him, the man said, 'Lord, I tried my best but the seed never germinated and I am really sorry'. On hearing this, the other people laughed at him.

Then to everyone's surprise the King proclaimed loudly, 'You will be my next Minister. What I gave to all of you, were steam-cooked and dried seeds, which cannot germinate. The rest of you cheated me by planting new seeds, when they found that they could not grow the original ones. I want an honest, sincere and trustworthy man as my minister - Congratulations for your honesty.' The moral of the story is that honesty is very important when we climb the ladder of success. Any employer will make sure whether an employee who is being considered for promotion, has three major qualities, namely, honesty, intelligence and an industrious nature.

When we study people, we see that although some are very intelligent and hardworking, they are not sincere. How can an employer promote such a one to higher levels and entrust him with more responsibilities? The future of the organization will not be safe in his hands. Again, we find that some others are sincere and intelligent but are lazy, and not ready for hard work. There is yet again another set of people who may be sincere and hardworking, but who lack intelligence. In my opinion, a perfect combination of honesty, a willingness to work hard, and intelligence, is tobe qualifying factor when we consider someone for a promotion. Although all these qualities are very important, I will give greater credit to the superior virtue of honesty. No wonder, this virtue has been exalted into the eminence of an adage: 'Honesty is the best policy'.

About the Author

he had never met before. Along with a charitable institution based in Kerala, The Kidney Federation of India, Kochouseph formed a kidney chain-the first of its kind in India, wherein he started the chain with his donation and one close relative of the recipient will donate her kidney and the next recipient's relative would donate further, thereby carrying forward this unique kidney chain.

His hobbies include listening to music, reading and watching documentaries in informative channels. He is married to Sheela who is heading and managing '*V-Star Creations*' the apparel division of V-Guard group.

The couple is blessed with two sons – Arun and Mithun. Arun is the Managing Director of 'Wonder La' and his wife Priya is the Executive Director of 'Wonder La'. Mithun is the Managing Director of V-Guard Industries Ltd and his wife Joshna is the Executive Director of V-Star Creations.

Now the second generation is actively involved in the family business and Kochouseph likes to spend a good amount of his time in philanthropic activities.

About the Author

Kochouseph Chittilappilly, was born in 1950 in Thrissur District, Kerala into a family which was traditionally engaged in agriculture. He holds a Master's Degree in Physics and began his career as a Supervisor in an electronics company.

At the age of 27, he started a modest SSI Unit manufacturing and selling stabilizers with just 2 workers. Now V-Guard is a listed company with various electrical, electronic and electro-mechanical products and the total turnover of group companies for the financial year 2010–11 was above 820 crores.

In the year 2000, he started an amusement park in the name '*Veega Land*', which has now become one of the most attractive destinations in Kerala. The success story of '*Veega Land*' made him to venture another amusement park, '*Wonderla*', in Bangalore, which is the biggest amusement park in India.

Kochouseph Chittilappilly is the recipient of numerous awards, which were bestowed on him for his exemplary performance in business. Kochouseph has authored a book, '*Practical Wisdom… in real life & management*' which exemplifies effective ways of practical management in business as well as real life, which he learned from personal experience and *Ormakilivathil* (Malayalam) – A true life memoir of his younger days.

He was also chosen as the Manorama – Newsmaker of the Year 2011.

Mr. Chittilappilly is also a humanitarian par excellence. He donated one of his kidney's to a poor and needy truck driver whom